W9-BME-571

THE
HELPING
RELATIONSHIP
Process and Skills

LAWRENCE M. BRAMMER / 5 7 3 ·
The University of Washington

Prentice-Hall, Inc., Englewood Cliffs, New Jersey

Library of Congress Cataloging in Publication Data

BRAMMER, LAWRENCE M
   The helping relationship

   Bibliography: p.
   1. Counseling. 2. Helping behavior. I. Title.
BF637.C6B676   361.3'2'019   72-12519
ISBN 0-13-386516-9
ISBN 0-13-386508-8 (pbk)

**PRENTICE-HALL SERIES
IN COUNSELING AND HUMAN DEVELOPMENT**
NORMAN R. STEWART, Consulting Editor

© 1973 by Prentice-Hall, Inc.
Englewood Cliffs, New Jersey

Printed in the United States of America

10 9 8 7

Prentice-Hall International, Inc., London
Prentice-Hall of Australia, Pty. Ltd., Sydney
Prentice-Hall of Canada, Ltd., Toronto
Prentice-Hall of India Private Limited, New Delhi
Prentice-Hall of Japan, Inc., Tokyo

Contents

Introduction

People want to be more helpful to one another. The basic purposes of this book are to describe a helping process and to provide a kind of road map for interested people-helpers to guide them in thinking through some relevant principles, skills, and research.

Although great progress has been made in material technology, we are still in the dark ages of human relations and exploration of human potentiality. Now that humans have substantial mastery over nature, there are indications that we want improvements in our relationships in order to be better parents, spouses, and generally more human. The growing popularity of applied psychology books, growth centers, parent education, sensitivity training, and voluntary services are ripples on the surface of the vast reservoir of desire to be helpful to others in some deeply human manner. Now that basic survival needs are satisfied, people are searching for deeper meanings to their lives through service to others.

Our basic problem is how to bring the existing vast resources for helping to bear on the equally vast human problems plaguing our society. We cannot depend solely upon helping specialists and human relations experts to close this large gap. A helping commitment must be encouraged and helping skills be widely dispersed in the population until such time as human satisfactions and better social organization makes formal helping, as we now know it, unnecessary.

While there is a need for specialists trained to cope with the complexities of human problems, most human needs can be (and have been) met by nonspecialist people-helpers. This book is written mainly for such nonspecialists who want a framework in which to view their helping functions, and for those who wish to join classes studying helping functions and skills in a systematic manner. Thus, people who work as generalists in counseling, group leadership, child care, youth work, teaching, rehabilitation, employment, police work, community relations, mental health, parent education, crisis centers, or church work hopefully will find the principles and techniques that follow applicable to their work settings. In addition to these special helpers it appears that about half of all jobs involve some type of human contact service, and this proportion is likely to increase. Therefore, all people with personal contact positions will find this book useful.

Persons in various consulting and instructional roles in community agencies and educational institutions will be able to use this book for in-service education on helping skills and human relations. Those persons following a programmed learning approach to human relations, communication skills, or counseling will find this text a useful framework for their skills training.

The thrust of this book is on helping normal individuals to function at a higher level. It is not a book on psychotherapy and the pathology of human interaction. I emphasize basic communication skill improvement, since a fundamental problem in all human relations is our difficulty in really reaching one another.

The two keys to the helping process are the helper as a person and his skills. This book focuses largely on the helper's task of developing into a more aware and effective person. He is first of all a human being, then a helping instrument in the form of parent, teacher, counselor, adviser, interviewer, or friend. Secondly, the helper needs precise skills to realize the outcomes people desire. These skills are presented in the categories of understanding, comfort, and action.

I have attempted to capsulize in simple form many principles and skills gleaned from twenty years as teacher, counselor, and behavioral science researcher in the people-helping realm. Yet, I recognize that the helping function can be enormously complex and controversial. We possess no neat body of valid knowledge about the helping process, but we have a good start. This book is an effort to describe this evolving process and to consider the helping process in light of changing social needs and diverse definitions of helpfulness.

I have kept citations, quotations, and technical terms to a minimum in my quest for clarity and simplicity. I have included, reluctantly, only a sampling of the vast helping literature from the helping professions. Suggestions for further in-depth study are included with each chapter.

I wish to acknowledge the helpfulness of Mrs. Winifred Raymond and Mrs. Jean Swindlehurst in the preparation of the manuscript. Thanks also go to my wife, Marian, for her patience and cogent suggestions from her experience as a teacher and parent.

1 | *Helping:*
What does it mean?

This is a book about people helping other people to grow toward their personal goals and to strengthen their capacities to cope with life. Few of us achieve our growth goals or solve our personal problems alone. We need other people in some kind of helping relationship to us; but what does this imply for helpers and the helped? This book is an effort to answer questions about the why and the what of helping others.

Help is a difficult process to put into descriptive words because it has such individualized meanings. It is necessary to understand the numerous meanings and implications of help, however, because all of us have work, community, or family responsibilities that demand helping relationships. This chapter is an exploration of these meanings. It is followed by an examination of some characteristics of effective helpers, theories about helping processes, and basic helping relationships. A detailed presentation of helping skills and action principles is made in the remaining chapters.

I will begin with a series of generalizations about helpers and helping as building blocks for the remaining chapters. These generalizations are primarily value statements and assumptions with varying degrees of demonstrated validity. There are very few statements one can make about this topic that are universally valid. Some are statements of belief

based on experience, and some are verified generalizations from behavioral science research. All generalizations I make here are intended
as thought and discussion stimulators and are presented to suggest some
limits to this vast topic. My principal goal in this chapter is to assist you
to think through and to extend your own views of the helping process,
because each helper must develop a style of help that is comfortable and
effective for him.

Outcomes you should expect from studying this chapter on the meaning of help are to be able to: (1) identify the basic points of view of this
book; (2) describe the essential nature of the helping process in terms of
need fulfillment and responsible independence; (3) list three arguments
which support, and three which refute, the professional and nonprofessional approaches to helping; (4) describe and illustrate self-help, peer,
cross-age, and community helper projects; and (5) list three sources of
personal gain to the helper from engaging in the helping process.

A formula for the helping process, for example, is illustrated in
Figure 1. The helper's personality combined with specific skills produce
growth conditions that lead to definite outcomes important to the person
and society in general. Whereas helper personality and skills constitute
the basic ingredients of the helping process, the specialist adds a third
element to broaden his awareness and to realize his helping potential.
He goes beyond the basics to an investigation of the recorded experience
of other helpers and the contributions of the behavioral sciences. He
formulates helping theories of his own. The more specialized helper also
asks questions about the value of his helping services and learns research
skills with which to answer those questions.

FIGURE 1. A formula for the helping process.

Personality of Helper + Helping Skills		= Growth-Facilitating Conditions	→ Specific Outcomes
traits	for understanding	trust	for the person
attitudes	for comfort	respect	for society
values	for action	freedom	

For purposes of this book the helping person will be designated as
the helper, and the helped, as the helpee. These are more generalized
terms for counselor–counselee, worker–client, therapist–patient, parent–
child, teacher–pupil, and interviewer–interviewee commonly used in
public agency and private practice settings. My underlying assumption
is that the basic interpersonal processes implied by these specialized
helping relationships are similar.

Helpee growth

Helping another human being is basically a process of enabling that person to grow in the directions he chooses. Help should be defined mainly by the helpee. This means that the helpee not only selects the goals of his own growth but that he determines whether he wants help at all. The helpee defines his desired help on his own terms. He may, for example, put his need in the form of requesting information, making a decision, solving a problem, or getting in touch with his feelings in a trustful relationship. We need to be aware, though, that helpees seldom admit directly that they want help. It is difficult to admit having a problem one cannot solve on one's own. Even when the helpee admits to himself that he has a problem, the degree of trust he feels will determine the extent of sharing it with a helping person.

This voluntary quality of the helping process is a crucial point since there are many persons who want to be helpful to others to meet their own unrecognized needs. Some helpers *need* "victims." Doing anything for another person without his initiative and consent frequently is manipulative and often is destructive. Even when the help is solicited and given with the best of human motives it may have an unplanned detrimental effect on the helpee. The reason is partly that the person being helped experiences a loss of self-esteem. Although appearing outwardly grateful, he may interpret the gift or act of help as a message that he is incompetent. This interpretation is accompanied by feelings of dependency, helplessness, inferiority, or inadequacy. He says to himself, for example, "Receiving this help makes me feel as if I can't take care of myself; I don't like leaning on somebody else." Such feelings often turn quickly to resentment or guilt. These common self-protective reactions are one reason the helping process has such unpredictable outcomes and why helping actions often are resented.

The underlying issue of this section is the amount of responsibility one should or can take for another person. Helpers vary over the full spectrum of responsibility from feeling a deep sense of human obligation to meet the needs of others to a view that others are totally responsible for their own experience and need fulfillment. The former group believes strongly that "I am my brother's keeper." The latter group claims that giving help perpetuates dependency and immaturity in the helpee. Help may vary over the entire spectrum depending on the circumstances. There are times when the human thing to do is to give total support to another without regard to dependency problems. Generally, however, the aim it to make the helpee self-sufficient; thus, bids for help and our inclinations to be helpful need to be scrutinized with this goal in the foreground. Important questions for the helper to ask himself are, "What is this person's capacity for independence and self-support at this time?" "How can I be supportive without reinforcing his dependency?" "What needs and rationalization prompt my own desires to be helpful at this time?" Chapter 2 contains a detailed discussion of helping motives and rewards for the helper.

A dilemma facing the helper is help for whom—the person or society? If the helper indicates by behavior or attitude to the helpee that he is looking after society's interests, he incurs his wrath and rejection. On the other hand, he cannot always support the helpee with the attitude that society is the enemy. The most helpful stance is to assist the helpee to see how his present behavior is shaped, for good or evil, by his environment. The aim is understanding, not blame.

There is a large amount of research evidence to support the claim that ostensibly helping relationships may be destructive, or at least non-consequential, for normal people, and for those pathologically inclined as well. This research has been surveyed by Carkhuff (1969) who concluded that the observed constructive results of the helping process were cancelled out by deteriorative results when the data were lumped together. When the average gains of the helped groups were compared with averages of the non-helped control groups, there were no significant differences. It is the difficult task of all serious people-helpers to look critically at their own helping behavior and the consequences for helpees' behavior to determine if their help was effective, ineffective, or destructive.

The act of helping a person with the presumed goal of doing something for him, or changing him in some way, has an arrogant quality also. This implication of superiority raises hostile feelings in the helpee because the act presumes that the helper is wiser, more competent, and more powerful than the helpee. Although these conditions may be true, as judged by external observers, the motive for help and the nature of the helping task as perceived by the helper must be made clear to the receiver.

The principle that the helpee must initiate the help request is confusing in another way. Must he always ask for help in words? A hurting child, for example, often cannot state clearly what he wants verbally, but his behavior, such as his expression and body tension, may be saying "Help me!" Our inferences from reading his behavior could be wrong; but the only way we can know is to respond, and then be alert to his reaction. A similar and unusual situation is the attempted suicide. The attempt may be interpreted as a desperate call for help. The idea that help must always be requested in clear terms certainly can be carried to extremes, particularly in situations that present danger to the person.

The aim of all help is *self-help* and eventual self-sufficiency. What I have emphasized here is that much of our growth is the result of self-help and self-searching, rather than a result of something done to or with us. Our needs for autonomy and self-actualization are strong, yet sometimes they are subdued temporarily by life experiences. These needs must be respected and strengthened for psychological survival, at least, and self-actualization, at best.

A further assumption I wish to include here is that each of us behaves in a competent and trustworthy manner if given the freedom and encouragement to do so. Sometimes this faith is shaken when working with people who have been hurt deeply by life and who thus behave in an untrustworthy manner. We must communicate to the helpee our faith and trust in his ability to move toward goals best for him and for society. This article of faith in the potential and desire of helpees toward growth is commonly held by most workers in the helping professions. In this discussion of helping I have stressed the significance of helpee *responsibility* for goals and self-determined growth, because this is the main purpose for helping.

We, as helpers, also must assume some responsibility by creating conditions of trust whereby helpees can respond in a trusting manner and can help themselves. Helpers do this through the *process,* a term which refers largely to their methods for bringing about helpee outcomes. These outcomes are realized through managing the environment, providing conditions for understanding and comfort, and by modeling trusting behaviors. A trusting approach means that the helper will view his task as facilitating and supporting, rather than as teaching or persuading.

While we are concerned with the helpee's inner world of feelings, values, and goals, we must be alert also to the impact of other people and of his physical environment. One implication of this view is that the helper needs to understand the special life circumstances of the helpee and to be where he is. The helper must get out of his office or agency sanctuary. Another implication is that a helpee is anyone who brings a matter to the helper's attention. This could mean a teacher or parent concerned about a child or a supervisor about an employee, as well as the person who asks for help directly for himself.

Helping by agreement

As a helping relationship develops, an important consideration is the nature of the agreement or "contract" between the helper and helpee. When help is requested outside of a friendship setting, it is important that the terms and conditions of the help be agreed upon early. Helpers get themselves into difficult situations in which they try more than they can capably or ethically deliver when the expectations of both parties are not explored and agreed upon. How this is done formally and informally will be described in chapters 4 and 8 under "structuring" and "contracting."

The nature of the agreement should be such that it implies a growth contract, that the helpee will try to change under his own initiative, but with minimal assistance of the helper. If the helper becomes preoccupied with the notion that *he* must help the other person, that *he* must produce some change, then the helpee has a demanding hold on him which could be very manipulative and destructive for both. Disturbed people with persistent adjustment problems often seek out such helping types; but they only frustrate their helper's efforts. The helpee in this instance is looking for something very idealistic or is demanding that something specific and unrealistic be given to him. The helper who falls into this trap reinforces the "helpless" or "sick" games of the helpee, thus preventing him from taking responsibility for helping himself. This topic will be expanded in later sections, but it is important for our introductory purposes here to realize the serious and complex nature of the commitment one makes as a helper.

Meeting helpee needs

Help consists of providing conditions for the helpee to meet his needs. Help varies (across a spectrum) from strong physical intervention, such as averting a suicide, to subtle emotional support, such as in a mild crisis. The kind and amount of help to give depends on the helpee's needs at the time. These human needs can be classified in various ways. A scheme that makes most sense to me was developed by Maslow (1962), and I offer it here as an example of a need system to understand the nature of help. Maslow arranges needs in a complex interrelated hierarchy of five levels according to their primacy in human existence. These five levels are *physiological, safety, love* and *belonging, self-esteem,* and *self-actualization.*

Physiological needs for sustaining life are so primary that until people have enough to eat, for example, any other form of helping is irrelevant. These physical needs are self-preservative and reproductive. Thus, helping means meeting a basic physical need such as food or clothing. For purposes of this book, however, helping processes will be restricted largely to acts of counseling, consulting, teaching, or facilitating satisfaction of psychosocial needs to be described below.

A second level of needs is for psychological safety, or ~ want to feel secure in our person. We want to know that our tu~ predictable. We are suspicious of change; and we want to reduce th~ tension from conflict, cruelty, injustice, and uncertainty.

The third level is love and belonging. We want to feel part of some enduring group where we are accepted, wanted, loved, and respected. When these conditions are reasonably satisfied, we can give love and respect to others. We then are able to show others we care and are interested in being helpful. If these love and belonging needs are not fulfilled in ourselves we tend to resort to numerous self-defeating or attention-getting behaviors, such as suspicion and aggression.

The fourth need level in Maslow's system is for achievement of self-esteem. To feel good about ourselves we need to be liked and regarded as valuable and competent by others. As we grow in awareness of our self-worth and get more in touch with our deeper needs, feelings, and values we depend less on others' judgments of our worth. The key implication here for the helping process is to find ways for people to think well of themselves, to believe in their competence and worth, through relationships with us.

A fifth need level exists that is difficult to define or describe. It functions best when the four lower levels of need are in process of being satisfied. It is a striving for self-development, integration, autonomy, stimulation, and challenge. It involves reaching out, often in risky ways, to move to higher levels of satisfaction and growth. This self-actualizing level of need helps to make sense out of much behavior that is not explained by deficiencies in need satisfaction.

The first four levels Maslow calls "D," or deficiency, needs. This person strives for fulfillment of a felt deficit, such as hunger, desire for love, or social response. Gratification brings a kind of calm and satisfaction, even depletion, for a time. Satisfaction averts the usual physical and emotional problems that deficits bring about. Yet what most people feel quickly after gratification is a vague craving for "something more." Maslow classified these needs for becoming more integrated, challenged, and individualized "B," "being," needs, to maintain a sense of high-level humanness and self-actualization. The person must do what he feels he can—paint, write, love, or serve.

The significance of need theory for understanding the helping process is that many requests for help come in the form of meeting deficiencies in needs for love, security, self-respect, or social stimulation. We need to help the person fulfill his basic physical and psychological needs before he can achieve higher levels of being and achievement. There would then be less need for people to meet their deficiencies in the form of crime, violence, and emotional distress.

This self-actualization need is paradoxical, however, in that self-actualization is achieved largely through helping relationships with people. Yet, Maslow's model of the self-actualized person was characterized by independence and self-sufficiency to accomplish these states with their own initiative and resources. In other words, it is possible that helping relationships beyond a certain point might retard the helpee's independence and self-esteem. This paradox translates into the assertion that the most helpful thing we can do for another person is to "help him help himself" by creating the conditions that release his powerful growth tendencies and abilities to use his own resources.

It is difficult for the helper to determine when a helpee is concerned about some basic need satisfaction and when he is asking for help with his dimly perceived striving for more creativity, autonomy, integration, or achievement. The helpee often has difficulty expressing what he wants, since all he experiences is a feeling of dissatisfaction with himself, uncomfortable feelings about his status, or awareness of meaninglessness in his behavior. He is aware that he wants something more than satisfaction of his appetites, as rewarding as this is to him.

In the process of exploring possibilities for his becoming more self-actualized, the "becoming" person discovers that his moment-to-moment satisfactions are occasionally punctuated with "peak experiences." These are feelings described by Maslow as transient states of being characterized by joy, delight, or even ecstacy. Thus, helping can be construed as a process of assisting the helpee toward higher levels of self-actualization and the joyful realization of his unused possibilities.

Helping can also be a process of achieving awareness of the conflict between the attractions of safety and comfort, on the one hand, and the risks and magnetism of growth on the other. Each condition has its delight and repugnance.

Universality of help

Helping is a function of all concerned human beings and is *not* limited to professional helpers. One of the significant developments in our specialized technical society is the professionalization of the helping process. Professional helpers realized, however, that they could not be all things to all people. Specialization became essential as a result of the professionals' sincere desires to maximize the delivery of quality helping services and to protect the unsuspecting public from unscrupulous or ignorant helpers who charged fees. The consequences of this development was to assign helping functions by custom and law to specialists!

One purpose of this book is to make some of the learnings of helping specialists more available to persons not having specialist responsibilities, and to encourage more widespread volunteer helping behaviors. Specialist helpers are far too few to make much of an impact; and it is a social tragedy to restrict these basic helping functions to a few specialists. This effort is not designed to minimize the contribution of specialists, nor to disparage their detailed skill and knowledge acquired in long, hard years of research, study, and practice. Meeting the health, psychological, and spiritual needs of dysfunctional people in our increasingly dehumanized society is so complicated and demanding that specialists will continue to be needed. These specialists should be used where and when their unique knowledge can be utilized more effectively. One problem with reliance on specialists, however, is that the person is a complex unitary organism. A specialized approach often ignores the needs of the whole person.

The overlapping functions of helping specialties is another confusing reality, since there are many labels for substantially the same helping process. The process, furthermore, has much in common with friendship. Schofield (1964) made an elaborate case for the fact that helping specialists offer a substantial amount of friendship to their clients. The irony is that these clients pay for this friendship which they should obtain in normal processes of living. It is a severe indictment of our culture that people must purchase friendship.

Science and art of helping

Helping is both a science and an art. The science portion involves elaborate research and theory on helping, mainly from the behavioral sciences, whereas the artistic aspects of helping refer more to the intuitive and feeling elements of interpersonal relationships which are based largely in the humanities and creative arts. The science portion is concerned with descriptive data, predictions, and generalizations about behavior. Nonprofessional helpers, although lacking this sophisticated behavioral science background and skill training, often can apply helping principles in their intuitive artistic fashion. One implicaton of the research to be cited below is to select persons as helpers who already possess these artful qualities, and then quickly and systematically give them basic helping skills and behavior concepts. I will emphasize this dual behavioral science and artistic approach to the helping function throughout this book.

Professionals and paraprofessionals

One of the main reasons for the increased employment of helpers outside of traditional professions is that data from some investigators, such as Carkhuff (1968), suggest that the effectiveness of professional helpers is much less than claimed or believed. These findings, coupled with data on the speed with which productive helping skills can be learned by nonprofessionals, suggest the desirability and feasibility of involving more such persons in the formal helping process. Rioch (1966) and Carkhuff and Truax (1965), for example, demonstrated the effectiveness of training nonprofessional adult helpers in mental health settings.

I would like to point out, as an editorial aside, that we have learned to depend heavily on experts in the helping professions, and we have allowed them to appropriate normal growth-producing processes into the mystical and sometimes exclusive domain of a professional guild. Too often elaborate professional entrance rituals are associated with a "divine right" to practice. This attitude leads frequently to interprofessional rivalries and jurisdictional disputes, such as those between psychiatrists and psychologists. This condition often puts guild welfare ahead of personal service. Laws have been passed, for example, that define psychotherapy and counseling and that designate who can perform these functions as a service to the public. Although designed to protect the public from unscrupulous fee-charging helpers, such laws also tend to constrict helping services. This is a dilemma that we must resolve soon in our society.

Helping-persons without the usual credentials sometimes are regarded as a threat to those with certificates and degrees in a helping specialty. Yet, it is sheer social folly not to utilize the untapped resources of helping talent in the nonprofessional population. Guerney (1969) makes a persuasive case for the use of nonspecialist helpers to meet manpower needs, particularly in services to children. Furthermore, there are abundant roles in training, research, and consultation for those helpers with more extensive and specialized skills and knowledge. The important consideration is who can be the best "significant other" to the person with emotional-social problems, and who can supplement parents and teachers with close sustained relationships to children. Many professional helpers, for example, depend upon verbal means of treatment help and thus limit their effectiveness to verbally facile

educated middle and upper social class people. Numerous persons needing help find direct nonverbal communication means more helpful.

Another variable is time. Usually the professional spends little time
with a helpee compared to others significant in his life. If these significant others received training in basic helping skills to supplement
whatever natural helping attitudes they had acquired in normal development, they might make an even greater impact on the helpee than a
whole clinic of professionals. The key question is, who can serve the
helpee most effectively? We must define effectiveness more precisely,
however, before we can answer.

Our society needs a "third mental health revolution," described by
Hobbs (1964) as an extensive and early preventive effort, coupled with
an expanded human potential movement to help people move to higher
levels of functioning. To facilitate this revolution we will need masses
of helping types of persons who are more available than the usual professional specialists, and who have confidence that we can change our
culture from basically exploiting to people-serving.

Many people have natural capacities to be helpful because of their
fortunate life experiences. They have the intellectual capacity to understand and nurture such natural helping characteristics so that they can
be even more helpful to others. I believe that many of these persons,
furthermore, have the capacity for insight into the destructive potential
of these natural helping processes if they are not used for the benefit of
the helpee. It is necessary, for example, that the helper become aware
of his power over others when he is helping, and how easy it is to abuse
that power unknowingly.

There are other severely limiting conditions for the nonprofessional
helper. He is subject to the same tendencies as the professional to distort his views of the helpee or to project his own problems to the helpee.
The nonprofessional possesses a great potential for distortion because
he is not as likely to be aware of this possibility as the professional
who goes through extensive supervision and training. The nonprofessional helper also is likely to pick up "contagious" feelings from the
helpee, whereas the professional has learned a kind of professional "distance" to counter this tendency. Both of these limitations can be greatly
reduced if the helper seeks or is assigned a supervising type of person
skilled in promoting a necessary kind of self-awareness.

Although this tendency toward emotional over-involvement can be
a limitation, it also has the potential for strength. For example, the
tendency for nonprofessionals to immerse themselves deeply in the emotional life of the helpee can be more facilitative of helpee growth than
the tendency of professionals to remain more detached. This complicated issue will be explored further in chapter 4.

In this era of accountability for outcomes, supervision from a professional can transmit an awareness of responsibility for what happens to helpees more readily. This ethical commitment to helpees and a sense of social responsibility are significant aspects of helper training.

I have been comparing the specialist professional with the generalist nonprofessional helper, but classifying helpers into these two categories is artificial and limiting. The professional helper earns his hard-won label through completing a prescribed program of training, meeting competency examination and licensing requirements, adhering to prescribed ethical standards, and being accountable for the outcomes of his help. Paraprofessional, on the other hand, is a term applied to persons with some of the skills and natural helping talents of the professional. They usually work directly with helpees under the professional's supervision, for training and agency accountability. A more descriptive term without the status implications of paraprofessional is needed, but this is the designation being used for the present time.

In agencies that utilize both professional and paraprofessional staff, issues soon arise over distinctive roles, client responsibility, essential qualifications, pay scales, and evaluation of helping effectiveness. Arguments and research around these issues could go on endlessly, but effective solutions can come about only with honest staff discussions of their respective strengths, limitations, and contributions. Each may be effective in meeting certain helpee needs and expectations, yet both helper groups are handicapped by helpee expectations that exceed current knowledge about the helping process. The basic problem, then, is matching helper self-perceptions of qualifications with helpee and agency expectations.

A second problem is determining and evaluating the complex variables that are assumed to be related to helping effectiveness. These variables are basic empathic qualities, knowledge of research and theory, skill performance, legal and ethical accountability to helpees and agencies, special knowledge from training or experience, and evaluation of competence by peers and professional associations.

Opinions in psychology and social work literature are divided between those who feel that paraprofessional helpers should function under close supervision as support and administrative personnel, on the one hand, and as independent helping persons on the other. By now it should be clear that my opinions support the latter view, providing due attention is given to the performance issues cited above.

Structured and unstructured helping

The formality of the professional helping process shades into various other levels as illustrated below.

Structured {

Professional helpers. (Examples: Social workers, ministers psychologists, teachers, school counselors, physicians, nurses, psychiatrists, legal counselors with specialized training and legal responsibility.)

Paraprofessional helpers. (Examples: Trained interviewers, receptionists, and aides in mental health, rehabilitation, and persons in correctional, educational, employment, and social agency settings.)

Volunteers. (Nonpaid persons with short-term training in basic helping skills and agency orientation.)

Unstructured {

Friendships. (Informal, mutual and unstructured helping relationships over time.)

Family. (Informal mutual helping system, interdependent in variable degrees.)

Community and general human concern. (Informal, unstructured, *ad hoc* helping acts to alleviate danger, suffering, or deprivation.)

The focus of this book is on the more structured forms of helping. Yet, it is striking to realize that formalized helping relationships in the form of counseling, treatment, ministering, or psychotherapy have characteristics in common with all effective human relating.

Community, peer and cross-age helping

Peer and cross-age helpers are additional applications of the helping principle. This is a condition where people of the same or similar age, or persons with similar problems, help others of comparable age or condition. An example is Alcoholics Anonymous where former problem drinkers help those wishing to reduce their drinking. Numerous forms of youth drug therapy and unwed motherhood programs exist where peers who experienced and solved similar problems are the helping agents. The New York Haryou program (*Youth in the Ghetto,* 1964), for example, is based on the idea that people not only meet their own needs to be helpful, but solve their own problems while helping others. The "Samaritans" is a movement in Great Britain consisting of volunteer unpaid helpers available at all hours to assist the lonely, distraught, and confused people in urban communities. They apply a kind of "first aid" at the time when people need the help most. The "Fish" program in the United States, which is organized largely around churches, has similar on-the-spot helping services. Most distressed people are not "sick" in a- medical sense, but ignorant, deprived, deficient, or abandoned by the community. It is a blot on our humanity that we cannot look after one another in helpful ways more effectively. The helping groups cited above are examples of progress being made toward solutions of these human problems.

In the educational setting the practice of pupils helping other pupils of the same or younger age is increasing. There are several studies verifying the utility of this method, such as those reported by Hawkinshire (1963). Here fourth graders with reading problems, for example, were assisted by sixth graders also having reading difficulties. While the fourth graders were helped to read significantly better, the helping process greatly enhanced the sixth graders' reading skills. Serving as a teacher-type of helper, therefore, holds great promise for helping others as well as for acquiring formal helping skills and knowledge to use in many contexts.

Varenhorst and Hamburg (1971, 1972) report the design and evaluation of a program to train youth from seventh through twelfth grades in helping skills for fellow students. These volunteers were given information about youth problems and referral resources along with training in interpersonal skills. The first evaluation indicated that this program was very effective in helping students with normal emotional and developmental problems.

Students at the adult level can become effective peer helpers as indicated in a community college study by Pyle and Snyder (1971). These students were judged to be very effective in helping fellow students with minimally essential support during the difficult transition to college life, handling dependency and autonomy issues, learning how to learn, and making curricular choices. Those students from ethnic minority backgrounds were helped especially by those who understood their background and problems of adjustment. As in other studies, a significant by-product was the personal growth of the student helpers.

It may be that persistent social problems can be alleviated by peer help also. In many major cities, for example, there is great concern among parents over busing children to achieve racial balance and to equalize educational opportunity. Among other reasons, one of the more covert is that many parents feel that their children will be held back if mixed with children of deprived educational backgrounds. If the peer helper principle and results mentioned above could be put into practice, it may be that both the accelerated and the less able pupils would benefit by a diverse classroom.

Perhaps children can be helped more by helping others than by following adult models or listening to others who are vastly superior to themselves. Although much work needs to be done on the usefulness of peer-helping relationships, enough is known to stimulate us to explore this helping resource more vigorously. A convincing rationale for use of young peer helpers has been given by Bruner (1972). He regards the intermediate generation of teenagers and youth as a new type of role bearer or model to bridge the gap between generations and to help youth and children make it into the adult world. Bruner thinks these young role models should be given more responsibility for teaching the younger, less experienced children on the grounds that they are key linkages between generations in periods of rapid change. This process could become an endless chain of helping, with the helped becoming helpers of others. The possibilities of peer-helper effectiveness in education, rehabilitation, mental health, corrections, and poverty programs are vast indeed.

Helpers gain too

Helpers change in the process, too, and they frequently are helped more than the helpees. It is apparent from the preceding evidence and discussion of peer helpers that the helpers can receive as much or more than the helped. The reasons for this are due very likely to the increased status and strengthened self-image of the helper as a result of being asked to help. Positive self-regard increases as a result of helping another person through giving rather than taking. Increased confidence in one's own psychological well-being comes from the awareness that "I must be O.K. if I can help others in need." The helping process, furthermore, takes the person out of himself and into the perceptual world of the other, thus diminishing concern with his own problems. Thus, sharing feelings is a behavior often resulting in strong mutual satisfactions for both. We need to recognize this strong need to be helpful to others and to provide more opportunities for volunteers to train and serve. The National Training Laboratories of the Institute of Applied Behavioral Science has recognized this need for encouraging volunteers and developing their skills by developing a Center for a Voluntary Society.

Riessman (1965) has surveyed the evidence in nonprofessional and peer-helper studies and has concluded that the benefits for the helper come from demands of the specific helping role, increased feelings of prestige, and awareness of new ways in which the helper is perceived and treated.

Riessman suggests also that placing persons who request help, such as drug users wanting to quit, in small helper roles starts a spiraling growth process whereby the helper's motivations for self-improvement and learning of helping skills gradually increase. Then he is added to the pool of people with high level helping skills to be shared with others. Thus, the "multiplier effect," illustrated above, is put in motion.

You probably recognize a paradox here. Whereas the helping process is ostensibly for the development of the helpee, we need to recognize the reality of the helper's needs for growth and satisfaction through the helping relationship also. This issue of satisfying mutual needs is so complex that more nuances of this topic are explored in chapter 4.

Self-help groups

There has been little research on why self-help groups are so effective in changing individual behavior. Hurvitz (1970) studied many groups as a participant-observer and concluded that much of their effectiveness was due to peer relationship among helpers and helped, inspirational methods, explicit goals, fellowship, and a variety of helping procedures. Hurvitz sees these helf-help efforts as more effective in many cases than professional psychotherapy. Self-help groups utilize many sources of help that are outside conventional helping methods. They depend heavily on charismatic leaders and often develop a religious or cultish atmosphere with demanding obedience to an authority.

A type of self-help group is spreading rapidly in America. While the groups cited above are organized around a specific need to change self-obstructive behavior such as alcoholism, hard drug abuse, or overeating, these groups are developed by people already functioning reasonably well in society, but who want to grow to higher levels of effectiveness. They are organized informally for purposes of spiritual and psychological growth, social enhancement, and mutual support in times of crisis. These functions formerly were supplied by the extended family or small church community, but these are now largely absent from the impersonal urban scene. I predict that this self-help movement will become a strong trend in our urban centers.

Helping is learning self-help

Helping is also a process of encouraging the helpee to learn how to learn. In the helping process the helpee not only learns more effective ways of coping with his present feelings and environmental demands, but he also learns techniques for solving his personal problems, methods of planning, and techniques for discriminating among value choices. Thus, a key meaning of the helping process is not only enabling the helpee to meet his present need, but to learn how to meet future needs as well. One of the most helpful services we can perform for another is to create conditions where he can learn how to solve problems with his own resources. There are a number of helper skills to bring this condition about which are described in chapters 5 through 8.

Outcomes you should expect from studying this chapter

After reading this chaper you can: (1) identify the basic purpose and point of view of this book; (2) identify the nature of help in terms of fulfilling needs and encouraging responsible independence; (3) identify three arguments supporting and three refuting the value of professional and nonprofessional approaches to helping; (4) describe and cite examples of self-help, peer, cross-age, and community helper projects; (5) identify three sources of personal gain to the helper from engaging in the helping process. We will now look at the personal characteristics of the effective helper.

Suggestions for further study

CARKHUFF, R. *Helping and Human Relations.* New York: Holt, Rinehart & Winston, 1969. (A two volume description of a model for developing helping skills.)

COMBS, A., AVILA, D., and PURKEY, W. *Helping Relationships: Basic Concepts for the Helping Professions.* Boston: Allyn & Bacon, 1971. (An overview of the helping relationship from a phenomenological viewpoint.)

————. *The Helping Relationship Sourcebook.* Boston: Allyn & Bacon, 1972. (A collection of readings from many authors on the helping process, mainly from a phenomenological view.)

FENLASON, A., FERGUSON, G., and ABRAHAMSON, A. *Essentials in Interviewing.* 2nd ed. New York: Harper & Row, 1962. (A general overview of the interviewing process, methods, and essential attitudes.)

ROGERS, C. "Characteristics of a helping relationship." *Personnel and Guidance Journal* 37 (1958); 6-16. (An early descriptive effort to define some dimensions of helping by a behavioral scientist.)

2 | Characteristics of helpers

There is a growing body of evidence that indicates that the person of the helper is as significant for positive growth of helpees as are the methods he uses. Effective and ineffective helpers cannot be distinguished, therefore, by their techniques, but they definitely can be contrasted on their personal beliefs and traits (Combs et al. 1969).

In this chapter I will focus on helper attitudinal characteristics and their implications, and in the following chapters I will cover methods for communicating these helping attitudes to helpees. Outcomes you can expect from studying this chapter are as follows: You will have competencies to: (1) list and illustrate six general characteristics of helpers and five facilitative conditions determined by helper personal traits; (2) describe five levels of functioning; and (3) describe the relationship between helper interview style and helper life style.

Combs and his co-workers studied some basic beliefs about people and self-help by contrasting various helpers from counseling, teaching, and the ministry with nonhelpers. The helpers perceived other people as *able* rather than unable to solve their own problems and manage their lives. People were perceived also as *dependable, friendly,* and *worthy*. Helpers had self-perceptions and traits distinct from nonhelpers, such as identification with *people* rather than things, adequate *capacity to cope* with problems rather than lack of problem solving ability, and more self-revelation and willingness to be themselves than self-concealing.

Rogers (1961) concluded from his experience and reviews of research that the helper's theory and method were far less important for an effective helping relationship than manifestations of the helper's *attitudes*. Rogers noted also that it was the helpee's *perception* of the helper's attitudes that made a difference in effectiveness. Research has confirmed what the life experience of most of us has indicated, namely that the helpful person needs to be an attractive, friendly person, someone with whom you feel comfortable, and someone whose opinions you value. (He inspires confidence and trust.)

Levels and styles of functioning

An important consideration in helping is the helper's level of functioning as well as the kinds of techniques he utilizes. Carkhuff and Berenson (1967) have described their five levels of functioning for each dimension which are very useful concepts for describing behavior of helper and helpee. Level 3, empathy, for example, refers to a minimum level of feeling response. Level 2, emotional functioning for a helper, means that he is performing at a level that detracts from helpee functioning, especially when the helpee is at level 3 or 4. Level 1 involves a very noticeable detraction from the feeling communication of the other with very little significant feeling communication going on. Levels 4 and 5, according to Carkhuff and Berenson, are significant additions to the communication of growth facilitative characteristics. The accurate expression and identification of feelings, and clarity of communication of the level 5 helper, for example, add to the helpee's ability to do the same. Respect or regard can be scaled similarly from the highest respect of stage 5 to negative regard of level 1. One implication of this levels concept is that in order to be helpful the helper must be functioning at a level higher than the helpee on the significant facilitative dimensions.

It would be simple if we could relate facilitative characteristics listed below to specific methods that the helper uses, but this condition is impossible at this stage of knowledge, especially considering the wide variations in style among individual helpers. The following facilitative characteristics embody elements of many divergent helping styles and theories. As a result, they have wide application to many helping relationships. Rogers, for example, stresses the essential contribution of helper personal traits to the broad helping process. Others, who emphasize behavior change, stress methods of changing the environment rather than helper attitude.

Carkhuff and his associates (1969) have presented convincing evidence that if the helper is functioning at a high level in regard to the following conditions constructive changes will take place in the helpee. The converse is true also that a low level of helper functioning can have destructive consequences for the helpee. Similarly, if the helper is functioning at the same level as the helper, no change is likely to take place.

HELPING AND HELPER LIFE STYLE

Another facet of the facilitative conditions described below is their natural outgrowth of helper life style. These conditions are not stylized traits that he turns on and off, but are characteristic of his life outside of the helping relationship. If he is not living these conditions he tends to be perceived as artificial and incongruous. The necessity to function at a high level puts considerable pressure on the helper to become and remain his own best self.

MATCHING HELPERS AND HELPEES

Although much research has been done on helper characteristics, helpee traits, and helping methods, very little has been done on the interaction of helper and helpee. There is growing evidence from research to support our common sense observations that the compatibility of helper and helpee personalities is a key factor in a successful relationship.

If we could match helpers and helpees on basic styles in advance we might produce more successful outcomes. For example, type "A" and type "B" helpers have been identified as having differential effects on helpees (Whitehorn and Betz 1960, Carson 1967). Type A is more "approaching" and interested in feelings, whereas type B is "less approaching" and is more cognitively oriented. Helping relationships of A types were characterized by greater trust, and helpee's were approached in a more active personal way than was typical of B types. In the near future it may be possible to develop training experiences that will match particular methods and helper styles with specific needs of helpees so that maximum outcomes can be achieved.

The helper personality

There is no cluster of traits that describes a people-helper who is universally effective. Research on counselor and teacher effectiveness indicates that although there is no fixed trait pattern for effective helping, there are strong indications of desirable conditions that facilitate constructive helpee changes (Carkhuff 1969, Combs 1969, Rogers 1961). I include the essence of these findings and their implications to serve as a tentative template of traits and behaviors that you can place on yourself. You must realize, however, that this list of characteristics is a composite from research and opinions of experienced helpers rather than a model of essential qualities and conditions for all helpers. I will present first some general helper characteristics, to be followed by a list of more specific facilitative traits and growth conditions created by the helper.

HELPER PERSONAL CHARACTERISTICS

There is a general dictum among people helpers that says that if I want to become more effective I must begin with myself. The reason is that our personalities are the principal tools of the helping process. Combs (1969) used the term "self as instrument" in the Florida studies. This phrase means that our principal helping tool is ourselves acting spontaneously in response to the rapidly changing interpersonal demands of the helping relationship. A teacher must react to new stimuli instantly, for example, with little or no thought ahead of time. How the teacher reacts is a function of who he is at that moment and how he sees his relationship with that particular student. We are behavior models for helpees no matter how we construe our helping role. They imitate our behaviors, identify with our views, and absorb our values. Although we may try to be an impartial and objective helper, the facts indicate that we cannot be such and still remain involved in the relationship. The following helper characteristics determine the nature of this relationship.

1. Awareness of self and values. There is universal agreement among practitioners and writers that helpers need a broad awareness of their own value positions. They must be able to answer very clearly the questions, "Who am I" and "What is important to me?" The reason is that this awareness assists the helper to be honest not only with himself but also with the helpee. He can say clearly, "This is where I'm at." This awareness also helps the helper to avoid unwarranted or unethical use of the helpee for his own need satisfactions. As I indicated in chapter 1, the relationship is a process of mutual need fulfillment, but the helper must know the limits of using the helping relationship for fulfilling his own psychological needs. Self-awareness provides some insurance, furthermore, against the tendency to project values to others. In every human relationship there is a fantasy of the other person that makes up a large part of our image of him. This fantasy consists of our values projected to him. For example, I may perceive the helpee from a few minimal cues as a very undependable person. The question is always, "How much of this judgment is really descriptive of him and how much is myself projected to him? Am I putting on him my own views of what is dependable? Dependability is a judgment; it is not a very descriptive term for behavior. Am I judging him against some vague social norm?"

While we may have opinions about traits of people we like and want to associate with, one characteristic of the effective helper is that he tries to suspend judgments of others. Although it may be helpful sometimes to confront helpees with our opinions, we should try to be descriptive of specific behaviors and to avoid labels mainly because so frequently they are projections of our own social values.

There are numerous helping situations that test the helper's values. If a helpee is describing a sexual behavior which the helper finds unacceptable to himself, or if the helpee is talking about divorce and the helper has strong convictions about the inviolability of marriage contracts, how does the helper behave? Can he maintain his own values and still accept the helpee? Can he empathize with the helpee, yet be keenly aware of his own values as a helper and his tendencies to project and judge?

How does the helper acquire the kind of awareness described above? Obtaining counseling for himself or participating in awareness groups are key sources of self-awareness. Reflection and meditation are other means. Self-renewal workshops which focus on examination of values and getting in touch with one's self are becoming sources of expanded awareness and renewed vigor to continue in demanding helping relationships.

2. The helper has feelings too. From observations of helping specialists an impression may be gained that one needs to be "cool," to evidence behavior characterized by detachment from feelings. While effective helping implies awareness and control of one's feelings to prevent the projection of needs described above, we must realize that the helper also is *feeling* all the time. He feels, for example, the elation of helpee growth toward independence. Similarly, he feels disappointed when his own expectations for the helpee's growth do not develop. He feels depreciated when his overtures of help are spurned by the helpee. knowing the reasons why helpee esteem needs require this kind of "rejecting" behavior is of some comfort, but helpers are inclined to respond with feelings of disappointment to others who do not value their efforts.

It is necessary to promote a feeling of confidence in the helper; and there seems to be a nice balance between the stance of the know-it-all expert and a self-effacing attitude such as, "I don't have any special talent or skill; I'm just little old me!" Am I aware, for example, of my tendencies to depreciate myself as a helper on the one hand, or my tendency to act like a "guru," one who has the answers, on the other?

Furthermore, why do I need to create a mystique about myself that promotes awe and dependency in the helpee?

As a helper I must learn to deal effectively with my confusion and value conflicts. When are self-assertion and expression of freedom important, for example, and when are conforming and adjusting the appropriate behaviors? The helper often is caught between liberating forces of growing independence and society's need to punish deviates, force conformity, and banish rebels. The helper must learn to live with this basic human conflict in himself and his helpees.

Feelings of power over helpees come quite unexpectedly. Unless the helper is wary, he is trapped into a smug controlling feeling when the helpee expresses strong dependence on him, or when he indicates that the helper has influence over him. When a helpee expresses profuse gratitude, for example, I begin to wonder if I really provided a condition in which he felt he helped himself, or whether he felt I did it for him. The latter feeling denies his own assertive self-help. It is like a child telling his mother, with some annoyance, "I don't need you anymore!"

Professional helpers label these unconscious feelings toward helpees as "countertransference effects," meaning that the helper's needs are expressed in behaviors such as dominating, overprotecting, loving, pleasing, seducing, or manipulating helpees. These feelings are "transferred" from the helper's own past relationships with significant people to the present helpee relationship.

The only known antidotes to the kinds of behavior described above are awareness of one's particular tendencies to "transfer" his own needs, problems, and unrecognized feelings to the helpee. This awareness can be obtained primarily through feedback about one's behavior in individual and group counseling experiences. Furthermore, one needs to have his personal life in such good order that he can take disappointment, frustration, demanding confrontations, and intensive encounters in helping relationships without projecting them to helpees, or developing personal symptoms such as depression, withdrawal, or physical complaints. As a helper one needs a strong "ego," meaning confidence in one's own worth as a person. Again, protections against self-defeating conditions are a counseling relationship for one's self occasionally and a satisfying personal life to provide continuous self-renewal. Helping is an emotionally demanding activity, even when done informally, and some provisions must be made for the helper to "recharge his own battery" occasionally.

3. Helper as model. The helper functions as a model to the helpee in the relationship whether he wants to or not. There is considerable support in the research literature for the power of models for acquiring socially adaptive as well as maladaptive behaviors (Sarason and Ganzer 1971). It is more controversial, however, whether a helper also must be a model of decorum, maturity, and effectiveness in his personal life. I have two reactions on this issue. The first is that the helper must have a fulfilling life himself, or he will tend to use the helping relationship too much for satisfaction of his own unmet needs. The second reaction is that the helper's credibility may be questioned if he has a chaotic personal life. If his marital life is stormy, for example, or if his children have constant brushes with police, the validity of his work is likely to be questioned.

The helper often is caught in the squeeze between his own self-fulfilling desires to deviate from local community norms and to resist pressures to conform, particularly if he is employed by local agencies such as schools and churches. Our society is reaching a point, however, where wide variations in behavior are more acceptable, and where the private life of the prospective helper is more respected. The final standard for judging the appropriateness of the helper's behavior is the helpee's judgment about the helper's usefulness in the present relationship.

Behaving like an "expert" helper in the eyes of the helpee is important to the helping relationship. Schmidt and Strong (1970) studied the behaviors seen as "expert" and "inexpert" from the helpee's viewpoint. Those helpers perceived as expert treated the student helpee's as equals with friendly attentive behavior. They spoke with confidence and liveliness. The "expert" helpers came prepared with knowledge about the helpee, his background and reasons for coming, and they moved quickly to the heart of the problem. Those perceived as "inexpert" were tense, fearful, rambling, uncertain, or overly cool and casual, communicating disinterest and boredom. Because of their more enthusiastic responsiveness to the helpees, the less experienced and less professionally trained counselors often were perceived as the "experts" by the student observers. To have influence with helpees, then, the helper must consider how he is perceived by the helpee and what kind of model he is presenting.

4. Interest in people and social change. A vital question for the helper is "Why do I want to help?" I stated earlier that the helper has needs too and that he can expect some kinds of satisfactions to maintain his helping behaviors. It is not too productive to engage in extensive self-probings about why one wants to help, but it is necessary to have some awareness of the fact that he is acting for himself as well as for some assumed value for the helpee. It is evident, however, that the effective helper is very interested in people. In his studies of effective helpers, Combs (1969) found that a central value was their concern with people rather than things and with an altruistic stance moving outward toward helping people rather than a more narcissistic focus on themselves. The effective helpers also identified with humanity rather than seeing themselves separated from people.

If helpers are asked "Why do you help," they are likely to come up with pious statements designed to impress others with their expansive humanity and virtue. Honest feedback from colleagues, friends, and helpers is a key source of awareness of motives for helping. Another is just to accept the probable fact that we have many basic needs and personal growth goals fulfilled by helping others. Such needs are self-worth, status, and intimacy. The standard for judging is the pleasure or pain experienced during and after a helping relationship, for example, "I just feel good about myself when I see people like Joe grow in social effectiveness." Just as some persons experience pleasure after creating a poem or playing a musical composition, so helpers experience a glow of satisfaction in experiencing human growth before their eyes and realizing that they had some part in facilitating this growth.

There appears to be a strong altruistic quality in helping types also. Granted, we could rationalize altruism quickly in terms of need theory or reward-punishment principles, but the love motive, in the Greek "agape" sense of non-erotic personal caring, is strong in helpers. They honestly feel that they are helping out of a deep love of humanity focused on a particular person. This motive has strong theological overtones and reflects the helper's profound commitment to a special view of the world and his place in it. Although I subscribe to a considerable portion of this kind of motivation for helping, I want to be sure my awareness "antennae" are tuned to feedback from the helpee so that I can check the validity of my views and the soundness of my motives. I want to know, for example, when my needs to convert others to my way of thinking and valuing, or to behave according to my model, become too strong.

It is my opinion that the Hebraic-Christian tradition has contributed in a solid way to the helping climate of our civilization. Yet, like knives, drugs, or machines, helping motives quickly can become destructive tools in the hands of naive or zealous users.

Findings from studies on altruistic behavior have some relevance here (Baron and Liebert 1971). Seeing a *model* of helping, that is, watching someone in the act of helping someone else tends to elicit this kind of behavior in the watchers. A strong *reciprocity* principle operates in altruistic behavior also. People tend to help those from whom they have received help, since our society has a strong "give and get" norm and a subtle system of social debts and credits. There is also a social *responsi-*

bility factor operating, since people tend to help those who are dependent upon them, even when the rewards for helping seem to be remote.

Interpersonal *attraction* was a principle operating in some of the helping studies. *Liking* the person and being of *similar background* promoted altruism. A compliance principle seemed to explain some behavior where helping was expected in order to obtain *social approval*. This is enough discussion to indicate that altruistic motives are extremely complex; and it is likely that a variety of socially conditioned as well as consciously chosen values motivate helping acts.

General helping acts often grow out of strong social support and change motives. From the standpoint of our collective self-interest, and perhaps survival as a race, it is essential that people function supportively to one another. When they do not, we are all jeopardized in the form of crime, accidents, and pollution. We must have more people concerned about the welfare of others if our society is to survive. This is the kind of condition that creates activist-helpers who are concerned primarily with changing social conditions to meet human welfare needs, rather than merely helping individuals to cope with the demands of an "ailing" society. A growing number of help-oriented people are seeing their function as change agents for large systems. Their goal is to create a people-serving and growth-facilitating society rather than to perpetuate destructive practices of present society.

5. Helper ethics. When personal beliefs about people and society become outlined clearly, they serve as conscious guidelines for action. When one values the helpee's welfare, for example, he will do nothing to harm him. If someone asks for personal information confided to him, he will not divulge it. He would regard that information as a symbol of trust.

When these ethical principles are shared widely among helpers, they become written down and codified. Professional people-helper groups have ethics codes. These codes are formal guidelines for action, and they reflect common values regarding helper-helpee relationships and responsibilities. The key value of a code to a helper is to give him some frame of reference for his own judgments about client welfare and social responsibility. For example, while his ultimate allegiance generally is to the society he serves, the helper's primary responsibility is to his helpee client. Information will not be revealed unless there is clear and imminent danger to the helpee or other people. The complexities and variations in circumstances make this topic too large for further discussion here; but hopefully it interests you sufficiently to delve into the details of ethical principles and codes among the suggested readings. The main point to emphasize here is that the helper becomes committed to a set of ethical behaviors that are reflections of his own moral standards, society's codes, and the norms of the helping professions.

6. Helper responsibility. Related to the helper's ethical behavior is the issue of how much responsibility he can assume for his own and his helpee's behavior. Responsibility is a judgmental term defined only in terms of a specific helping context; but there are common understandings about responsible helper behavior. The helper behaves ethically, as defined above, meaning that he balances helpee welfare and social expectations. He knows and respects his personal limitations so that he does not promise unrealistic outcomes. He refers helpees to specialists when his limitations and their needs so dictate; and the helper maintains contact until the specialist takes responsibility for a new relationship.

The helper defines his relationship to the helpee in a manner clear to the helpee. There is a clear norm among professional helpers that should, in my opinion, apply to all types of helpers. This norm says that once a helping relationship is agreed upon the helper will do all in his power to make it productive until such time as a transfer of responsibility is made to another helper, or until either person voluntarily and formally terminates the relationship.

The issue of how much responsibility a helper can or should take for a helpee's behavior is very unclear. Some helpers move to one extreme of saying that the helpee is the only one responsible for the outcomes or consequences of the relationship. Others maintain a very accountable stance under the assumption that the helper is mainly responsible for what happens to the helpee as a result of the helping relationship. It is my observation that most authorities view this issue as a shared responsibility. They keep this question open and move along the responsibility continuum according to their best judgment of the specific condition and age of the helpee. The helpee is responsible for his own decisions, for example, including how much of himself he is ready to reveal. The helper is responsible for presenting ideas, reactions, or support as deemed appropriate or as requested by the helpee.

There is a misperception about responsible behavior in regard to helpees revealing personal data about themselves. There is the common (and questionable) assumption that if the helper just listens to the helpee this can do no harm; but listening has a powerful uncovering effect on the helpee. He often pulls down his protective psychological armor while he becomes more open. The effect on the helpee is often a feeling of vulnerability and hurt, or sometimes fear over having revealed too much. Responsible helper behavior is knowing when to "cap off" these self-revelations, or expressions of feeling. One of the great dilemmas of helping is that we can't be helpful if the helpee is not open, yet the most helpful thing we might do is assist him in limiting his self-revelations.

HELPER AS SCHOLAR-RESEARCHER

The thoughtful helper soon realizes that he must have some framework for ordering his experience with helpees, some way of thinking about what he is doing. When he begins to question his assumptions about people, the effectiveness of his helping approach, or the validity of helping in general, he is *thinking* like a behavioral scientist. When he collects data systematically about his helping behavior, makes valid inferences, generalizes carefully, and forms conclusions about those data, he is *acting* like a behavioral scientist.

The critical helper sees the need for more information about the process, more effective skills, and more useful theories about people and the helping function. So he turns scholar by reading about others' experience in helping and the results of specialized research reports related to his interests.

Although not all helpers can or should become behavioral science researchers, they need to have the critical thinking and observational skills of the scientist. The actual research techniques for validating procedures and discovering new knowledge are part of professional helper's education, but even they tend to leave the bulk of formal research to specialists. All people-helpers are scholars though, in the sense of reading and applying results from helping books and journals.

While research evidence (Joslin 1965) and experience indicate that one can be an effective helper without extensive formal education, the helping function draws upon the ideas and raises many questions related to the disciplines of philosophy, biology, psychology, sociology, and anthropology, as well as literature and the arts. In other words, the helper's possibilities for flexibility and effectiveness increase as his own cultural awareness expands. He must be committed, in any case, to the idea of life-long learning to avoid obsolescence and to maximize his helping effectiveness. He expresses this commitment in the form of a reading program, feedback on his skills, and personal development.

As the helper becomes more involved he develops increasing interest in the social context of helping. He finds, for example, that the helpee's background as a social minority member, an immigrant, or a resident of a particular urban subculture has a profound effect on his helpee's outlook and life style. Understanding his background provides a sounder basis for empathy, understanding, and interventions in the helping relationship.

THE HELPER AS A GROWTH FACILITATOR

Since the principal helping function stressed in this book is facilitating achievement of helpee growth goals, I will present some of the supporting data for goal facilitator characteristics. This helper role is different from more traditional models of helping. These alternate approaches are, first, the *priest model,* which focuses upon conducting ceremonials, interpreting sacred writings, and providing spiritual support. His help consists of supporting, prescribing rules for living, and providing outside intervention. His goals are to make one's lot in this life more effective, and to prepare for the next. Another model we all know well is the *medical approach* where diagnosis of complaints and application of treatments are the key features. The helpful elements are being told what is wrong and being given treatment, surgery, or prescriptions for correcting the disease condition. The *behavioral engineer model* stresses management of the environment. His help consists of changing the physical and psychological environment to meet essential human needs. Although these descriptions are oversimplications of other helping models, they are cited as contrasts to the *growth facilitator model* of helping.

The principles cited in Chapters 1 and 2 are descriptive, in part, of the growth facilitator approach. Stress is placed on the personal characteristics of the helper reflected in behaviors that facilitate helpee psychological growth. This personal approach, coupled with the methods of behavior change technology, seem to offer the most effective approach to helping.

Rogers (1957) specified six essential conditions for helpee development. Although there has been controversy over whether Rogers' conditions are essential and sufficient, there is wide agreement that the helper conditions he cites are very desirable. Most helpers agree, for example, that positive regard is important, but few assert that this regard must always be *unconditional* to be helpful. Rogers' conditions are *congruence* (meaning consistency and genuineness) in the relationship, *unconditional positive regard* for the helpee, *empathic understanding* of the helpee's internal frame of reference, and efforts to *communicate* this understanding. Several investigators over the past few years have checked the relationship between these and other facilitative traits with helpee behavior outcomes. Some of the more productive studies are those of Truax and Carkhuff (1967), Combs et al. (1969), and Carkhuff (1969). Results of these and similar studies are described in the remainder of this chapter.

1. Helper empathy. Empathy is the principal route to understanding helpees and enabling them to feel understood. The helper sees the world the way the helpee perceives it, that is, from his "internal frame of reference." The helper makes an active effort to put himself in this internal perceptual frame without losing his own identity or objectivity. He does this largely by thinking *with* rather than *for* or *about* the helpee. The word empathy derives from the German word "einfülung" meaning "feeling into." It is related to the kind of response that sports spectators give when they lean forward with the jumper. Similarly, helpers tend to "feel into" the helpee's feeling experience as he talks.

The helper tries to become an alternate self for the helpee, a kind of emotional mirror. Thus it is an enabling condition for the helpee to experience and use what the helper is offering. The main criterion of success for helper empathy is whether the helpee can use the helper's empathic understanding for own self-understanding and consequent confidence in his ability to solve his own problems or to make wise decisions. To function at a minimum level, the helper must respond accurately to covert feelings as well as to the overt content. Briefly, then, the helper manifests empathy through his ability to perceive what is going on in the helpee's feelings and to communicate this perception clearly to the helpee. Figure 2 illustrates these internal and external frames of reference.

FIGURE 2. Internal and external frames of reference.

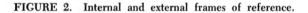

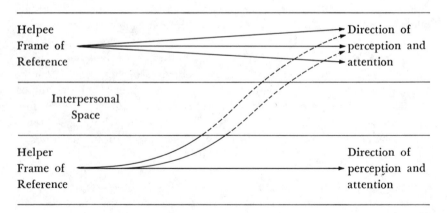

The helper gets into the internal frame of reference by listening attentively and asking himself several questions. "*What* is the helpee *feeling* right now? *How* does he view this *problem*? *What* does he see in his *world*?" If the helper is thinking from an external or diagnostic frame of reference, he is asking "why" questions as, "*Why* is he so upset? What is *causing* the problem?" He also makes judgments such as, "He's *upset* and seems to be in bad shape; I've got to help him." The external frame, then, is the helper's attempt to understand the helpee from an observer stance using an intellectual problem-solving framework. Combs (1969) found his effective helpers used an internal rather than external framework for perceiving their helpees. The external may be an appropriate approach for some stages in the helping process but not when the goal is to understand helpee feelings.

Since so much helping is done over the telephone in crisis centers and informal counseling, the question of face-to-face contact for empathy is significant. A study by Dilley, Lee, and Verrill (1971) in which face-to-face, confessional type, and phone contacts were used found no differences in helpers' ability to communicate empathy in the three methods. This kind of study suggests that more helping could take place effectively over telephones.

In figure 2 the helper and helpee are moving along their respective perceptual tracks such that the helper tries to think and feel like the helpee. The helpee must be sufficiently open to allow the helper to direct a high proportion of his attention and emotional energy toward his goal of getting into the helpee's framework. This condition is difficult to achieve, particularly in helping situations in which the participants are far apart in race, age, experience, or socioeconomic status (Brammer and Shostrom, 1968).

The converse condition of too much empathy on the helper's part could be a problem too, such as, perpetuating a dependent kind of immaturity. As illustrated in figure 2 the helper maintains a sense of independent direction in his own perceptual track as he attempts to get within the helpee's framework. If he moves too fast and too completely into the helpee's frame, he is likely to lose his objectivity and sense of direction. Through this overidentification with the helpee he is likely to be perceived as more sympathetic than empathetic. Even when the helper maintains a strong empathetic stance there is the ever-present likelihood that the helpee's problem becomes the helper's burden too!

2. Helper warmth and caring. These related terms refer to key emotional response qualities in the helper. Warmth is a condition of friendliness and considerateness manifested by smiling, eye contact, and nonverbal attending behaviors. Showing concern and interest such as offering the helpee a chair, looking after his comfort, and making him feel valued are also means by which to show warmth.

Caring is a term closely related to warmth, but it is regarded as more enduring and intense emotionally. It means showing deep and genuine concern about the welfare of the helpee. The act of caring has strong affectional overtones also, meaning that it is a way of saying "I like you."

Some helpers speak of warmth and caring as mild types of non-possessive love for the helpee which meet his needs for response and affection. Early in this century Freud and his followers emphasized warmth as a significant factor in therapeutic power. Warmth in the helper conveys a personal kind of psychological closeness, as opposed to professional distance.

The helping skill involved here is how to convey this feeling of closeness, affection, and caring concern to the helpee without emotional entanglements, offensive forwardness, or threat. Some helpees, for example, have been so hurt by life that they cannot deal effectively with warmth when proffered, so the alert helper will adjust his behavior to reduce the threat. Neither will he be embarrassed or upset when the helpee responds with cool detachment. In some social groups if one gets emotionally involved with another, it makes him vulnerable to rejection and obligates him to the person offering the warmth.

A second helper concern is how much warmth to exhibit at different stages in the helping process. Although the helper does not turn his warmth on and off, he is aware of the facilitative or debilitative effect of his emotional behavior on the helpee, and adjusts accordingly. For example, showing warmth and caring are especially helpful in the early stages when the relationship is being built. They are helpful also when the helper is going through a crisis, where the supportive value of helper warmth is especially desirable. Professional helpers for the past 60 years have written about the importance of warmth for a productive helping relationship. It is only recently, however, that research results have supported the facilitative effects of warmth and caring (Truax and Carkhuff 1964).

3. Helper openness. One of the principal goals in the beginning of a helping relationship is to encourage the helpee to disclose his thoughts and feelings freely to the helper. This self-disclosure is related to the helper's openness, since he must be willing to reveal where he is in reference to the helpee in an honest way. Combs (1971) found that effective helpers were able to use self-revelation in building a constructive relationship. The essential condition of trust, furthermore, is directly dependent on the extent to which helper and helpee are open to one another.

Like so many helper characteristics, openness is paradoxical in that too much self-revelation on the part of the helper confuses the issue as to who is helpee and who is helper. A helper needs to be aware when his needs begin to supersede those of the helpee. The only general guideline that I can suggest for deciding how much self-revelation is appropriate, is that the helper reveal only enough of himself to facilitate the helpee's self-disclosure at the level of functioning desired. The helper reveals himself in a progressively free manner natural to a developing relationship. Too rapid disclosure on his part may overwhelm the helpee with unexpected behavior or threaten him with too much personal data.

A term that Rogers (1961) and other writers utilize in this context is *genuineness.* This is a state where the helper's words are congruent, or consistent with, his actions. If the helper says, for example, "I'm glad to see you," he reflects this feeling with body language and voice quality consistent with his words of welcome.

Another word used in helping contexts is *authentic*—the opposite of phoney. The helper tries not to hide behind a professional role or facade. A certain amount of social game playing behavior may be appropriate early in the process when the helpee meets the helper and expects conventional behavior in saying hello and ascertaining the helpee's expectations. The helper concentrates on listening and trying to understand what the helpee is feeling so that he can respond with appropriate and authentic feelings. The helper uses discretion in expressing negative feelings about the helpee at this stage, however, since such expression may be destructive to him.

Carkhuff (1969) distinguishes between two stages of genuineness. The first involves a low level of functioning in recognition of the natural way trusting relationships develop. The helper is also in a *responsive* set, listening to the helpee. In the second stage of genuineness, the helper is in an *initiative* set where he is more freely himself as a person, thus enabling the helpee to be more expressive. Carkhuff emphasizes the modeling effect of the helper in this stage where he sets an example. The open quality of communication exhibited by the helper leads to an honest sharing and encountering type of relationship where the helpee learns to be more open and genuine.

Congruence is another term used in helping professions to express the correspondence between the helper's behaviors, such as his words, and his basic attitudes (Rogers 1951). Congruence refers also to the helper's credibility. He is perceived as more believable when his behavior and attitudes appear to "ring true" to the helpee. Perceiving the helper as congruent facilitates the helpee's congruence between his own words and feelings because of the modeling effect described above. When the helper, for example, says he is interested in the helpee's problem, his words should be consistent with his basic feelings; otherwise the discrepancy will be apparent to the helpee. The consequences very likely would be loss of confidence in the helper or annoyance at the helper's feigned interest.

4. **Helper positive regard and respect.** This characteristic is an attitudinal set that expresses not only the helper's deep concern for the helpee's welfare but also respect for his individuality and worth as a person. Rogers (1961) expressed this condition as "unconditional posi-

tive regard" meaning a nonjudgmental, "no-reservations" attitude. It says to the helpee that he is free to be himself and that he will be respected for it. The literature on helping, shows that the term "unconditional" appears to be controversial. It means literally no conditions or judgments that will hamper the helpee's expression of feelings or ideas. I consider unconditionality relative to stages in the process of helping. In the first contacts it is important to convey through acceptance and warmth the attitude that "I neither approve nor disapprove of what you are saying. I want you to express yourself freely, and I will respect your right to feel as you please and to act as you feel within the limits of our mutual welfare. I want you to become your most real and effective self. Furthermore, I want to be with you because you are a person."

Later in the helping process, when the relationship is well established, the helper begins to experience a variety of feelings toward the helpee. Then the regard becomes more conditional. The helper becomes more expressive of his own approving and disapproving attitudes, thus tending to reinforce or diminish certain behaviors in the helpee. The helper's spontaneous and authentic behaviors become more apparent as the trust level deepens and the helpee is more open to honest feedback from the helper.

The principal vehicles for expressing regard and respect are words matched with genuine nonverbal expressions of warmth, acceptance, and empathy. The helper conveys the attitude that his help is being given with the condition that the helpee express honest feelings and attempt to become his best self on his own terms. He is not required to please or conform to the wishes of the helper. This respectful stance is facilitated by conscious efforts to be freeing rather than controlling or manipulating. Combs (1969) found such an approach was used effectively by the helpers in his study.

5. Helper concreteness and specificity.   A key facilitating condition for accurate and clear communication in helping is the helper's attempt to be specific rather than general or vague. He models concreteness, but he also confronts the helpee about specificity and clarity. When dealing with painful and unacceptable feelings there is a tendency to be abstract and circuitous to avoid direct confrontation with those feelings. Painful feelings tend to be stated in vague and elusive language in the beginning. In this instance the helper may say, for example, "You appear to be uneasy; most people seem to be uneasy in new situations." Another example is, "Please give me a specific example of what you feel right now." The strategy is to confront him with the request for *his* specific and present feelings stated in concrete terms. Using general phrases, such as "most people . . .," "they say," or "it seems we . . ." detract from the specific personal reference desired in the form of "I feel . . ." or "I think that. . . ."

The helper assists the helpee to focus more on present, rather than past or future, concerns and feelings through questions and reflections. The helper also models good examples of specific communication by using clear "I" statements. That is, he speaks in terms of "I think . . .," or "I feel . . .," rather than "People say . . .," or "They think that. . . ."

One problem in using and encouraging specific expressions is that they may tend to reduce the spontaneity and free association of helpees' expressions of feeling. So often helpees wander about in vague circuitous fashion, tapping sensitive areas cautiously. This issue must be resolved by the helper according to his best judgment. Typically, he might encourage and model specificity and concreteness of expression early in the process. Then when the helpee becomes more involved, allow him more freedom to express himself in his natural verbal style. Finally, when the process develops to the point of planning specific courses of action and when it demands a problem-solving approach, greater emphasis can then be placed on specificity and concreteness of expression and action.

A concluding statement

After reviewing the ideal helper's personal characteristics, one is struck with their paradoxical *simplicity,* yet *complexity,* for facilitating growth in helpees. Most of the conditions described in this chapter are extensions of ordinary effective human qualities. The relevant research and cumulative experience of professional people-helpers points out the necessity, however, for examining continuously the amount and timing of these growth-facilitating conditions for a particular helpee at a particular moment in his development.

Also important is the need to be *flexible* as a people-helper. At times one must be deeply personal, immersing himself in the relationship, and at other times must be an objective observer, studying the process carefully. He must be able to move freely along the full range of these facilitating characteristics so that he can respond appropriately to helpee needs at different stages in the helping process. On the one hand this must be a natural intuitive process, an artistic creation, and on the other hand it needs to be a deliberate rational process of sizing up and meeting helpee needs. Although this artistry comes naturally to some, it is most often an outcome of intensive and extensive effort and criticism.

However one construes the helping process—primarily as an art or basically as a science—it is essential that the serious helper take periodic looks at the assumptions he makes about himself, his helpees, and the helping process. This chapter focused on the helper as a person and how he uses his personhood as a helping tool. In the next chapter we will explore his functioning as a thinking being who reflects on his work and develops a rationale for his help. Various models are presented for developing a productive method of self-criticism and for describing what he is doing and why he is doing it.

Outcomes you should expect from studying this chapter

You can: (1) name three research investigators of helper characteristics and cite their key findings; (2) list six general behavioral characteristics of helpers; (3) cite and illustrate five growth-facilitating conditions for helping relationships through helper personal qualities and values; (4) describe the close relationship between helper interview style and helper lifestyle. The final criterion of successful mastery of the ideas in this chapter is your demonstrated ability to live a whole and creative life in and out of your helping relationships.

Suggestions for further study

AMERICAN PSYCHOLOGICAL ASSOCIATION. *Ethical Standards of Psychologists.* Washington, D. C.: American Psychological Association, 1953 (Proposal for modification: "Standards of ethical behavior for psychologists." *American Psychologist* 13 (1958); 266-71.)

BRAMMER, L., and SHOSTROM, E. *Therapeutic Psychology: Fundamentals of Actualization Counseling and Psychotherapy.* Englewood Cliffs, N.J.: Prentice-Hall, 1968. (Ch. 6 on characteristics of the therapeutic psychologist.)

ETHICAL STANDARDS, AMERICAN PERSONNEL AND GUIDANCE ASSOCIATION. *Personnel and Guidance Journal* 40 (1961); 206-9.

HAMECHEK, D. *Encounters with the Self.* New York: Holt, Rinehart & Winston, 1971. (A comprehensive survey of principles and research findings on development and understanding of the self, especially Ch. 7 on developing a healthy self-image.)

ROGERS, C. *On Becoming a Person.* Boston: Houghton Mifflin, 1961. (A collection of Professor Roger's papers on various personal aspects of the helping function.)

3 | *Thinking about the helping process*

The helper functions as a person while in contact with the helpee. Thinking is part of the helper's personhood. There are times during the helping process itself when the helper evaluates what is going on, but generally in his more private times he is a thinker about and evaluator of himself, the helpee, and the helping process.

Theory as a guide

As used here, theorizing refers to a rational rather than a feeling function. The helping person needs a guiding theory to help him make sense out of the complexities in the helping process. A person certainly can be helpful to others in ways described in chapter 1 without a thought about theory, but if he is going to work systematically in a helping function, he needs some "hooks" on which to hang his experiences and some frame of reference for gaining perspectives on his work and improving his services. His theory then becomes a set of useful guiding principles. This chapter describes then the need for such a systematic way of thinking about helping and the principal ways other helpers have described their work. The two outcomes you

can expect from studying this chapter are to: (1) identify some guidelines for thinking about your own theory of helping; and (2) describe
contributions of the major categories of current helping theory.

Each helper must develop his own style and theory about helping.
He cannot simply take the ideas of another person and make them his
own because he has not had the same life experiences or ways of looking at people. He may find others' assumptions similar to his own, but
each helper must take responsibility for revamping them into his unique
ideas and beliefs. Freud was not a Freudian and Rogers was not a
Rogerian. Each was himself, and each built upon the wisdom of the
past. Their admirers, often in true discipleship fashion, gave their own
explanations of the helping process a Freudian or Rogerian label.

The helper builds his theory through three overlapping stages.
First, he reflects on his own experience. He becomes aware of his
values, needs, communication style, and their impact on others. He
reads widely on the experience of other practitioners who have tried
to make sense out of their observations by writing down their ideas
into a systematic theory. In this sense, theories are a sophisticated form
of common sense. Finally, the helper forges the first two items together
into a unique theory of his own. If he writes his ideas in systematic
form, gives them a label, and attracts followers, he may even become a
founder of another theory of helping!

There is no one preferred helping theory. Each approach to more
formal counseling and psychotherapy has limitations and strengths for
explaining the events in the helping process. We are a long way from
a generally applicable theory of helpfulness. The data from research
studies and observation of students in practice reveal the impressive
effectiveness of numerous styles and approaches. Although helpees generally are fair judges of what is effective with them, their judgments
are not the final answer either. Some helpees profess to be helped by
tea leaf readers, magicians, and other types of "helpers" with mystical
and extravagant claims.

A personal theory of helpfulness

CONSTRUCTING A THEORY

Basically, a theory should be a rationale for what one does in the
name of helping. It should include basic assumptions of how people
learn and change their behavior. It should have some element of how
personality is put together (structure), how it develops (growth), and

how activity is generated (motivation). My own theory of helpfulness contains a *philosophical* dimension that includes my values and expected outcomes. It is a statement of the kind of person who should emerge from the helping process—an ideal growth model. Theory has a *structural* dimension that provides a kind of cognitive map for looking at the person totally, and specifically at his current stage of growth. It is a scheme for helping to picture how the helpee's personality is organized. A *developmental* dimension is important to help differentiate the helpee's various normal and deviant growth stages as he moves from dependence to independence, from incompetence to competence, and from simplicity to complexity. Finally, there is a *process* dimension that helps to explain how the person learns and modifies his behavior. For example, people learn in two basic modes. Some persons need to experience something first and then reflect on the learnings—experiential learning. Others need to understand it and see all the parts first and then do it—cognitive learning. Occasionally, some use a trial-and-error process and seem to stumble into answers to problems, or insights emerge unexpectedly—discovery learning. Each of us has a style that works best under a given set of learning requirements, and our basic task in learning how to be helpful to others is to discover our most effective learning style.

As you think about your own theory of helpfulness, the following selected questions should be considered:

1. *Values and goals:* What is my view of the "good life"? What is my model of an effective, well-functioning, mature person for existing in our society at the present time? What do I want for this life? What is my responsibility to others?

2. *The nature of humanity:* How is the human personality structured? What motivates him to behave as he does? How do thinking processes take place? What are the relationships among thinking, feeling, and valuing? How does man make choices? Does each person create his own life, or does each live out the history of the race in an unique way?

3. *Behavior change:* How do we learn? Do we change the environment first, or our personality characteristics first, and then expect behavior to change? Do we act first, then learn; or do we obtain understanding first, then act? What does it mean to be helpful to another person?

The questions listed above contain profound philosophical issues over which people have been arguing for centuries. Some are religious in that they require a declaration of faith. Others are empirical, meaning that research can help with the answers. In any case, they are illustrative of the complexity, depth of thought, and length of time required to develop a comprehensive working theory about people and the helping process. For more detailed suggestions for developing a personal theory and for more specifics about my theory, see Brammer and Shostrom (1968) in the suggested readings list at the end of the chapter.

USEFULNESS AND LIMITATIONS OF THEORY

A theory of helpfulness is useful when it enables one to describe and explain what he is doing in a helping relationship and why he is doing it. Theory is an intellectual tool to systematize and simplify the complex observations one makes continuously. Theory should help us fill in spaces in our perceptions that may be missing or vague, as we do when we put pieces in a puzzle. The process helps us in making choices of technique. If our theory focuses on rational problem solving, for example, we will utilize more rational methods, such as problem analysis, in our helping. If our theory stresses the significance of feelings, we will tend to focus on clarification of feeling states as a means to help.

If we have a theory with the elements described above, we should be better able to explain helpee behavior. If the helpee, for example, is exhibiting unusual avoidance behavior while making a choice among alternative solutions for his personal problem, we can make some guesses regarding his fear of commitment or taking risks of failure. Our theory may give us leads or informed hunches on why people resist choice or change. These hunches also serve as research leads which can be verified with more precise and extended observations. So, our theory should push us to seek new knowledge through research.

The basic limitation of all theories, however, is that they are generalizations from observations of particular helping situations. When they are reapplied to an individual, one must be very careful not to oversimplify the situation or explain it away with a theoretical generalization. For example, our theory may indicate that generally the helper's self-revelation generates helpee self-revelation and that this is an essential condition to move the helping process forward. This generalization must be applied carefully to avoid destructive consequences of too much helpee self-revelation.

The principal value of the thinking process we have labeled theorizing is that the helper can *systematize* his observations so they make sense to him. As a result, he can *communicate* his ideas about the helping process to others.

General theories of the helping process

As described above, helpers tend to develop their own theories. For some persons who operate rather intuitively, their theory is a simple statement of key assumptions. Others couch their theories in complex technical writings which at times seem to be mystical and even cultish. Students and followers of past writers developed "schools" that were named after the person who wrote about them, such as Freudian, Sullivanian, or Rogerian. Descriptive titles such as psychoanalytic or behavioral, for example, are used more frequently now. The following outline lists some key features of the principal approaches currently in use. Such on outline has all the risks of oversimplification and biased selection, but the following summaries are presented here as an orienting overview to classification, contributions, and limitations of helping theories. Detailed information about numerous specific theories must be obtained as early as possible from the suggested readings section.

ECLECTIC VIEWS

Most helpers tend to have an eclectic orientation. This means that they take a broad and flexible view on the critical questions about personality structure and behavior change. Eclectic helpers utilize concepts, techniques, and assumptions from many viewpoints. An eclectic view does not include casual picking and choosing from many different theories, a practice that has brought eclectic views into bad repute in some professional groups. It is a difficult theoretical stance to adopt because of the hard work required to integrate many complex ideas along a broad spectrum of helping functions.

Eclectic views must be consistent, as well as comprehensive. There appears to be renewed interest in a sophisticated type of eclecticism that emphasizes development of one's own personal theory of helping. It is still stylish in professional helping circles, however, to identify with a particular psychonalytic, behavioral, or phenomenological view.

PSYCHOANALYTIC

The psychoanalytic view has the longest history and most complex set of assumptions and structures of all the helping theories. The essential idea is that understanding one's psychosexual life history is crucial to working through personal problems and achieving normal development. Later psychoanalytic writers emphasized social learning as opposed to genetic influences in development. It postulates a life energy that is stored in a location of the personality called the unconscious. The intrapsychic conflict among the various forms of energy expression in the person are the sources of human problems. Psychoanalytic theories are known as depth views because of their emphasis on life history factors and involvement of various levels of personality structure. The levels are ego (mastery), id (impulses), and superego (conscience). A key contribution of psychoanalytic theory to the helping professions is the idea of defense mechanisms whereby the personality seeks its internal stability by defending itself against disintegration within and attack from without. The principal means for helping a person under this system is a process of working through his developmental problems into the present. One of the main limitations of the psychoanalytic view from the helpee viewpoint is that he gets the impression that his problems are caused by intrapsychic conflicts and that these conflicts arise out of his past history. These conditions, then, are considered to be beyond his present control and responsibility for doing anything about them. The methods of helping used in his approach are long, arduous, and unpredictable. Equally lengthy and demanding training is required of helpers who wish to use psychoanalytic methods.

PHENOMENOLOGICAL

The phenomenological view of helping focuses upon the uniqueness of each person's perception of reality. The helper is understanding to the extent that he can get within the phenomenal world of the helpee and see things the way he perceives them. The emphasis is on the present rather than the past or the future, and so how he feels about himself and his world now is the crucial consideration. This view includes a cluster of theories, some of which emphasize a self as the main perceiving instrument. Sometimes these views are called *self-* or *client-centered* theories because of the focus on the person and his perceptions of himself. A key assumption is man's drive toward growth and integration.

A related helping theory is *gestalt,* which emphasizes confrontation with self in the reality of present time. This view stresses honesty and openness in encounters with other people as the basis for helping and personal integration. Broadened awareness is one of the principal goals of gestalt helpers.

A cluster of phenomenological viewpoints known as *existentialism* is attractive to people-helpers because of its focus on humanness. Existentialism is a philosophical outlook speaking to issues of time, meaning, purpose, feelings, and the human potential.

The main limitation of phenomenological and gestalt theories is their high degree of subjectivity, which leads to vagueness, mysticism, and problems of research.

BEHAVIORAL

Although most of the theories mentioned so far emphasize inferred subjective states such as feelings, the behaviorally focused helper concentrates on objective observation of behavior. There is keen interest in learning as a form of behavior change. In this sense all helping in the form of formal counseling is behavioral in that learning or changing behavior in some form is the basic process. The main differences appear in explanations of how behavior changes and in the degree of emphasis put on outcomes in helpee behavior rather than on process. For the behavioral counselor the function of reward is very important because much evidence exists for the principle that behavior that is rewarded tends to be repeated. If one wishes to increase the helpee's search for information to help him solve his planning problem, for example, he must see that his information-seeking behavior is rewarded in appropriate ways.

Behavioral helpers stress specific and concise goals, such as developing an educational plan or making a choice among two potential marriage partners. The main standard of success for the helper is the degree to which the helpee reaches his stated goals. This emphasis on precision of goals and measurable outcomes is an attractive feature to helpers with a behavioral set. Research on counseling processes and outcomes is made much more possible in the behavioral framework largely because observable behaviors are the variables studied.

The principal limitations of behavioral views are the difficulties in dealing with feelings through observable behavior. The emphasis on specificity, precision, and objectivity tend to lead the helper to focus on minute pieces of behavior and to ignore larger complex patterns.

EMPIRICAL-RATIONAL

Related to the behavioral approach is a cluster of viewpoints stressing *rationality*. Thinking processes are therein examined and corrected by pointing out faulty logic and assumptions to the helpee on the assumption that altering his belief system leads to changes in his behavior. A helper using this approach would tell the helpee that his difficulties in making choices, for example, seemed to be due largely to his catastrophic expectations. Seeing clearly how he was distorting his thinking would remove this obstacle to positive action. A teaching role, therefore, is one of the principal helping functions.

A large group of helpee problems revolve around making plans and choices that require information about oneself or the world of reality, like work. Educational-vocational planning of youth is an example. Here the emphasis is on rational *problem solving* and prediction of success in a given training event. Sometimes this viewpoint is known as the *trait and factor* theory because the focus of effort is assessment of personal traits and intellectual factors. This task of assessment is accomplished mainly through psychological tests that can predict success in study or work. Helpers stressing this viewpoint do not deny the significance of feelings in human events, but they tend mainly to focus on the more observable rational events in the helping process. Computer technology is being tapped as an adjunct to the helping process where information and prediction are special needs.

The chief limitation of rational approaches is a disproportionate emphasis on rational and observable behaviors to the detriment of that vast influential and irrational feeling realm of existence.

TRANSACTIONAL-COMMUNICATIVE-REALITY

The group of transactional-communicative-reality theories focuses on communication patterns among the interested parties, such as parent and child, or teacher and pupil. A study is made of the interactional patterns and the mechanisms people use to influence, manipulate, and reach other people. The assumption is made that each of us carries within himself remnants of child, parent, and adult communication patterns. The helping process consists of examining these patterns, and in particular the distortions of these states of being between individuals. One form of distortion, for example, is the "game" the helpee is playing with himself and others. Helping is facilitated by training in communication skills so that intentions are matched with behaviors. Feelings, as well as thought patterns, are considered. Much responsibility is placed on the helpee for his own choices and actions. The helpee is taught that he is responsible for his own behavior, meaning that he must "own" his own problems rather than blame others. This theoretical framework is used extensively with family problems where communication patterns are complex, rigid, and distorted. The principal limitation of this cluster of communication approaches is its limited set of assumptions about behavior; a more comprehensive view usually is required to deal with the complexities of family problems.

PHYSIOLOGICAL

Although there is no general physiological category among helping theories, there is a strong emphasis in helping interviews and groups on body awareness, sensory awakening, and brain wave functions. The basic idea is that many of our difficulties in living effectively result from the fact that we have lost touch with the physical dimension of our existence. We deny our impulses, dilute our sensory awareness, and ignore messages from our bodies. Much of helping effort is devoted to enriching life through reawakening the senses, opening awareness to our bodies, enjoying physiological processes, and utilizing knowledge of alpha brain waves to promote relaxation and self-understanding. Methods used are relaxation, breathing control, fantasy, massage, touch, and feedback control of brain waves. Much of this kind of training is conducted through growth centers such as Esalen Institute. In the United States alone there are over 130 such growth centers.

Outcomes you should expect from studying this chapter

When a helpee comes to me and says, "I have a problem and I want help," this statement of need usually translates into, "I am unhappy with the way things are; I want to change . . .", or "I want to decide . . . ;" my theory of helping is basically an explanation of how one sees this process of change taking place and where the focus of effort needs to take place. As one's helping theory develops, he experiences increased awareness of his understanding of the process and increased ability to explain his views and describe his observations to others.

The major outcome you should have achieved by studying this chapter is that you have thought through your own ideas about helping. You have the beginnings of your own unique theory. As you thought about developing your own theory you had three options I recommended the third of the following choices as the principal way to develop a personal and flexible approach to the helping process: (1) You could continue to help others intuitively without thinking too much about your implicit assumptions. (2) You could learn thoroughly one of the current approaches described above and apply it systematically. (3) You could develop your own unique viewpoint in the eclectic fashion described above.

Secondly, you have an overview of the major categories of theory which you can use as a framework for reading about specific theories. The most important outcome from this chapter is improved judgment about the use of theory and research flowing from it, as a means to affect your helpee's behavior constructively.

Suggestions for further study

BRAMMER, L. "Counseling Theory." *Encyclopedia of Education.* New York: Macmillan, 1971. (Ideas for developing a helping theory.)

————, and SHOSTROM, E. *Therapeutic Psychology: An Approach to Actualization Counseling and Psychotherapy.* Englewood Cliffs, N.J.: Prentice-Hall, 1968. (Chapter II on overview of theories, their contributions and limitations; Chapter III on an eclectic theory.)

FORD, D., and URBAN, H. *Systems of Psychotherapy.* New York: Wiley, 1963. (Detailed analyses and critiques of the major approaches.)

KRUMBOLTZ, J. "Behavioral Counseling. Rationale and Research." In *Behavior Change in Counseling: Readings and Cases,* edited by S. Osipow, and W. Walsh. New York: Appleton-Century-Crofts, 1970. (Overview of behavioral approach to helping.)

PATTERSON, C. *Theories of Counseling and Psychotherapy.* New York: Harper & Row, 1966. (Detailed survey of major writers on helping theories.)

ROGERS, C. *Client-Centered Therapy.* Boston: Houghton Mifflin, 1942. (Description of client centered and phenomenological views.)

STEFFLRE, B., ed. *Theories of Counseling.* New York: McGraw-Hill, 1965. (A series of papers by different authors on the major theories of counseling.)

4 | *The helping process*

This chapter is intended as a map through the complicated pathways of helping. It will list typical sequential events in the helping process and cite some of the problems encountered at each stage. Methods for dealing with these stages will be covered in chapter 6 through 8.

Outcomes that you may expect from reading this chapter are competencies to: (1) describe the dimensions and steps in a typical helping process; (2) list the functions of a helping relationship; (3) act more confidently when facing some of the problems encountered in the various stages; and (4) develop your own cognitive map of the helping process on which you can place your ideas and methods about help. The ultimate criterion of successful study of this chapter will be your ability to transform understanding of how to initiate, maintain, and terminate a helping relationship into demonstrated competence to do so.

As implied in chapter 1, the helping process takes place in a relationship. More formally, this relationship takes the form of an interview. The interview is merely a structured helping framework in which two persons are involved. When there are more than two in a helping relationship, we define it usually as a helping group of some type, such as an encounter, counseling, therapy, or training (T) group. These variables are sketched in figure 3. To think of a helping group, merely expand the number of helpees and change the interview label to group process. The term *process* refers to the on-going events and their meaning in the interview or group.

FIGURE 3.   The helping relationship in the interview.

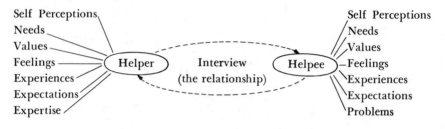

Relationship

The helping relationship is dynamic, meaning that it is constantly changing at verbal and nonverbal levels. The relationship is the principal process vehicle for both helper and helpee to express and fulfill their needs. The relationship is the chief means for meshing helpee problems with helper expertise. Relationship emphasizes the "affective" mode, because relationship is commonly defined as the inferred emotional quality of the interaction.

DIMENSIONS

Brammer and Shostrom (1968) listed the main dimensions of a helping relationship. One is *uniqueness-commonality*. Helping relationships generally are unique among human interactions. They have common features, yet they are as diverse and complex as the persons involved. An aspect unique to helping relationships, for example, is the helper's unusually extensive acceptance of the helpee. On the other hand, helping relationships have much in common with friendships, family interactions, and pastoral contacts. They are all aimed toward fulfilling basic human needs, and when reduced to their basic components, look much alike.

Another dimension is the relative amount of *intellectual and emotional content*. A relationship can be primarily an emotional encounter between two people where no words are spoken, or it can contain a heavy intellectual exchange about the helpee's eligibility for services from the helping agency. Helping relationships typically range over the full spectrum of feeling and thinking. Usually there is a progression of emotional involvement that proceeds from an initial level of attraction, to deeper friendship, through increasingly more involvement in a true encounter. This deepest level is characterized by full loving concern for the other's welfare. An important implication for helpers here is to be aware of the *level* of emotional involvement taking place and the consequences for the helpee of such involvement. The optimum level toward which to strive depends upon the goal. The helper, on the one hand, can be so detached and intellectual that he is perceived as distant, disinterested, or afraid of feelings. Yet, if the helper allows himself to become too emotionally involved he may lose his objectivity and develop relationships such as those experienced by lovers or parents and children. Helpers need to deal comfortably with this paradox of involvement. They need to maintain their objectivity, so they remain in reasonable control of their own feelings, know what is going on in the relationship, and yet remain enough of an emotional participant to keep the helpee involved at an appropriate feeling level.

The dimension of *ambiguity-clarity* contains another concept. It refers to the perception of the helping relationship as vague or structured. Initial ambiguity allows the helpee to project his own needs, concern, and feelings into the relationship without constraints; whereas, if the relationship were structured initially as a precisely focused interview, the helpee would be inclined to respond to the narrowly perceived purposes of the helper. If the relationship were too ambiguous in terms of purpose and identity of the helper, the helpee would be likely to react with considerable anxiety, or would drift into social conversation. The key to resolving this dilemma is that the helper and helpee must decide what this helping relationship is designed to accomplish and choose a level of ambiguity consonant with this purpose. If the purpose, for example, is to explore helpee feelings or to discover what is on the helpee's agenda, leave the relationship and your helper role deliberately ambiguous so he can use the relationship as a screen on which to project his feelings, ideas, and goals.

A crucial relationship dimension is that of *trust-distrust*. Helpees are willing generally to accept help from people they trust. The helpee must have confidence in the helper and must be able to believe what he says in order for trust to develop. Trust is a relationship condition that accompanies certain specific helper behavior that helpee's perceive as trustworthy. An example is clear motives for helping. The motives of the helper must be apparent and attractive to the helpee. They must not be a cover for helper efforts to control, manipulate, or punish. The helpee perceives himself as being accepted and valued as a person. He feels warmly received. He perceives the helper as sincere in his efforts to give of himself and his willingness to reveal his own feelings honestly. The helpee experiences the relationship as a shared and confidential effort to achieve growth, as a mutual problem-solving and learning activity. Yet, the helpee can feel free to accept or reject the relationship and the implied help. These conditions are necessary to establish readiness in the helpee to accept help.

Conversely, distrust is inevitable when offers of help are resented or rejected. This is often the case when the helpee thinks the reason for help is to change him. The helpee may feel dependent, inferior, helpless, or depreciated; thus, he resists the helper. This becomes a circular event since the helper senses his resistance and feels unappreciated and possibly even rejected. This condition often sets in motion more intensive, but veiled, retaliatory efforts to change the helpee, or it results in cooling and eventual termination of the relationship with residual feelings of disappointment or anger in both persons. One of the most insidious guises for helping another person is the helper's rationalization that he is acting for the helpee's own good, whereas in reality he is doing it for manipulative or punitive reasons to fulfill his own needs.

Little research has been done on trust. Two studies have given us a clearer picture of the nature and effect of trustworthiness. Strong and Schmidt (1970) studied the effect of perceived trustworthiness on the helper's influence. They used interviewers trained in trustworthy and untrustworthy behaviors. Trustworthy behavior was defined as showing genuine interest in the helpee as well as absence of ulterior motives, nonconfidentiality, and boastfulness. It was difficult to produce roles characteristic of significant untrustworthy and trustworthy behavior in this study, but they did clarify the nature of the trusting process. In later research Kaul and Schmidt (1971) studied the factors influencing perceptions of trustworthiness. They found that the interviewer's manner had a more significant impact on his perceived trustworthiness than did his words. The key implication for our discussion of the trust dimension here is that we must attend more to the effects of our nonverbal communication. What we tell with our bodies is related to our genuineness and honesty. Kaul and Schmidt's definition of a trustworthy person was one who respects needs and feelings, offers information and opinions for the helpee's benefit, generates feelings of comfort and willingness to confide, and is open and honest about his motives. Trust also came from the reputation of the helper and his position which denoted trustworthiness.

There are other dimensions related to levels of personal-social responsibility, freedom-control, and ethical commitment, but these have been discussed in earlier chapters. This section is an introduction to some of the general dimensions and relationship problems. The following discussion will describe, in more specific terms, two additional conceptual schemes for understanding the helping process. The first is an overview of the process as experienced typically by both helpee and helper. The second will list the specific stages in a typical model of the helping process. This list will be followed with more detailed descriptions of problems encountered and general strategies for meeting them.

The helping process as experienced

The following sequence of events is typical of helpers' and helpees' experiences of moving from first contact through final outcomes. This general sequence is not dependent on helping style or theory of helping. It is an unfolding of a natural process of problem solving. Note that in Figure 4, the helpee's feelings, questions, and interpretations of what is going on are matched in parallel form with those of the helper. The process moves typically from an *initial statement* of a problem by the helpee, to a covert translation of that problem or concern into a broader awareness of the *underlying message* he is trying to give the helper. Then he moves to a further translation of the problem into a *goal* he wants to reach, on to an awareness of his need for a *problem-solving process,* to experiencing the helper's *strategy* and *method* for reaching the goal or solving the problem. Finally, he experiences the *outcomes* themselves. This sounds like a complicated and stylized process, but it is experiencing a natural movement toward a goal, fulfilling a need, or solving a problem. The helper goes through a parallel process of experiencing *initial questions,* then forming some preliminary *inferences* and *hypotheses* about what is going on. Making *agreements* with the helpee follows. Finally, the helper chooses a *strategy* of helping, and experiences movement toward the *outcomes.*

Stages in the helping process

The stages listed below are typical of the process, but they do not always exist in this exact sequence, nor are all stages always present. Helpee approaches to the helping relationship often determine the sequence and length of stages. Some helpees, for example, come with very vague requests, sometimes just with an uncomfortable feeling; whereas others come with specific requests, thoughtful expectations, and much experience. Some help takes the form of specific skill development, such as

FIGURE 4. The helping process as experienced by helper and helpee.

HELPEE BEHAVIOR

Initial statement of concern.

How do I state my desire for help?

"I need help . . ."

"I have a problem . . ."

"I'm unhappy . . ."

"Something is wrong . . ."

"I can't perform . . ."

"I can't decide . . ."

Can I trust this other person?

What am I getting myself into?

HELPER BEHAVIOR

Initial questions and reactions.

Why is he here?

How does he see his present situation?

What is he feeling and thinking?

How does he perceive me, and this relationship?

What is his world like?

What does he want of me?

Initial statement translated into a basic message.

I can't cope with the demands of myself, of others, of the situation.

I need more information, more skill, more love, more understanding . . .

Formulating inferences, hunches, and hypotheses.

What messages is he trying to convey?

I see his basic problem as . . . Is this valid?

Can I meet his expectations?

What additional information do I need to explore?

FIGURE 4. (Cont.)

HELPEE BEHAVIOR

Statement of a goal (usually in the form of "I want . . ." statements).

I want to decide . . . do . . . plan . . .

I want to feel more confident . . . worthy . . . happy . . .

I want others to like me . . . notice me . . . change to . . . get off my back . . .

Awareness of process needs.

I want a relationship to explore my feelings.

I want specific information about . . .

I want to talk over my various choices . . .

I want more choices to consider . . .

HELPER BEHAVIOR

Peliminary inferences and judgments about helpee need.

The helpee needs a process—planning, problem solving, decision making.

The helpee needs a relationship to work through feelings or obtain support.

The helpee needs information.

The helpee needs referral for specialized help.

Making an agreement or contract to meet helpee expectations.

I will (can)—

give information.

give time to listen.

give support.

I will not (cannot)—

relate to this person.

meet his expectancies.

I expect the helpee to—

do his agreed part.

take responsibility for any decisions or plans.

FIGURE 4. (Cont.)

HELPEE BEHAVIOR

Experience helper's strategy and methods.
I meet with the helper for the agreed purposes.
I experience what we are doing as helpful (or not helpful) as evidenced by . . .

Outcomes experienced.
I feel better about myself.
I feel better about others.
My skills have improved . . .
I feel better about my situation . . . .
I enrolled in . . .
I obtained a job as . . .
I experienced myself as competent in . . .

HELPER BEHAVIOR

Choosing a strategy of helping.
I choose specific interviewing methods to meet helpee needs.
I look for feedback from the helpee on the effectiveness of my help.

Outcomes perceived.
I experience myself as helpful to this person.
I see specific behaviors he has learned, courses of action he has chosen, or plans he has made.
I hear stated feelings he has experienced.

relaxation. Other help takes a more cognitive form—acquiring information, making a decision, solving a problem, or making an educational and career plan. Often help is requested for managing intense feelings or resolving interpersonal problems. These diverse helpee needs and problem statements, therefore, call for some variation in the stages.

Another variable determining the sequence and emphasis given the stages in the helping process is the theoretical outlook of the helper. If he takes a strongly behavioral stance, as described in chapter 3, he will construe the process as unfolding in a certain manner. He would see it quite differently from a gestalt helper's conception of the process of helpee growth. The helper leaning in the behavioral direction would see the process as discovering the problem, establishing the behavioral objectives, describing the interventions, managing the environment, evaluating the behavior change, and following up. The gestalt approach to process, by contrast, focuses upon establishing the relationship, expanding awareness and self support by use of confrontational methods, and enabling the helpee to decide on a course of action growing from the awareness of self and others. Both views emphasize the outcome of personal responsibility for decisions; but the behavioral view stresses the process of managing the external environment, whereas the gestalt and similar views emphasize the process of changing the internal environment (awareness).

From a generalist helper point of view, there are eight stages in the helping process, as follows:

1. Entry: Preparing the helpee and opening the relationship.
2. Clarification: Stating the problem or concern and reasons for seeking help.
3. Structure: Formulating the contract and the structure.
4. Relationship: Building the helping relationship.
5. Exploration: Exploring problems, formulating goals, planning strategies, gathering facts, expressing deeper feelings, learning new skills.
6. Consolidation: Exploring alternatives, working through feelings, practicing new skills.
7. Planning: Developing a plan of action using strategies to resolve conflicts, reducing painful feelings, and consolidating and generalizing new skills or behaviors to continue self-directed activities.
8. Termination: Evaluating outcomes and terminating the relationship.

You may note that the above sequence is a general model of the helping process which is designed to incorporate problem-solving, skill-development, life-planning, and awareness models.

The goals of this stage are to open the interview with a minimum of resistance, lay the groundwork of trust, and enable the helpee to state his request for help comfortably and clearly. Helpees come to a helping relationship with mixed feelings. On the one hand, they want whatever the helper has to offer; yet there is a strong resistance in even the most highly motivated helpees. *Resistance* is a standard term in counseling literature used to denote the helpee's defensive reluctance to begin a helping relationship as well as his covert thwarting of the goals of the interview, once the process is underway. There are several reasons for this resistance. In the first place, cultural norms in certain segments of society construe seeking help as an expression of weakness or incompetence. We are expected to handle our problems with fortitude and common sense, and so there is reluctance to get involved because of this cultural pressure to be independent.

Much resistance comes from within ourselves due to our tendencies to resist change. We talk glibly about growth and becoming more effective people, but we really do not want to work up to our potential by going through the discomfort of change. The following interview excerpt illustrates these points.

Hr: You seem to be just sitting there. What is that doing for you?
He: Well, I can't seem to get going. I don't want to work today.
Hr: You don't really want to help yourself, then?
He: Well, yes I do, honestly, but then again, I'm scared.

Fear of confronting one's feelings is a strong deterrent for seeking help. The pain must be great in most of us before we will admit that we need a helping relationship. We may try all kinds of substitutes like drugs, for example, first. It is important for helpers to recognize this ambivalent, or mixed, feeling in all helpees.

We must recognize also that even those who have made a clear commitment to seek a helping relationship use all kinds of stratagems, of which they are unaware, to resist changing. This process also takes place long after the helping relationship is underway. The helper constantly needs to devise methods for dealing with resistance, such as confronting the helpee with his behavior as in the illustration above. The helpee may, for example, discuss matters at a high intellectual level to resist facing his feelings.

Helpers frequently ignore the milder forms of resistance, since they are protection for the helpee against intense feeling experiences. As the trust level develops resistance tends to diminish. Another focus of the helper therefore, should be on what he is doing to build the trust level of the interview. At some point the helper must ask what in his own behavior is contributing to the helpee's resistance. Other forms of managing the resistance levels of the interview are described in the references at the end of this chapter.

The helper should realize some of the realities of a new relationship:

1. It is not easy to receive help.
2. It is difficult to commit one's self to change.
2. It is difficult to submit to the influence of a helper; help is a threat to esteem, integrity, and independence.
4. It is not easy to trust a stranger and to be open with him.
5. It is not easy to see one's problem clearly at first.
6. Sometimes problems seem too large, too overwhelming, or too unique to share them easily.

To assist the helpee to determine his readiness for a helping relationship, the helper needs to remind himself that before a helping process can begin effectively, the following helpee conditions need to prevail:

1. Awareness of feelings of distress.
2. Desire for a change from the present situation or behavior. (He wants to help himself.)
3. Awareness of the potentials and limitations of a helping relationship.
4. Voluntary desire to see a helper.

Setting. The setting has something to do with ease of starting a helping relationship. This is an individual matter and should be an honest reflection of the helper's style. The kinds of clothes he wears, the appearance and decor of his room, and the opening conversation should reflect his nature and style. Most helpers agree with the obvious suggestion that distractions and interruptions should be eliminated; but, here again, helping can take place anywhere.

Even the distance of the chairs, assuming the helping is conducted while sitting, should be such that it facilitates communication and comfort. Distance between chairs generally varies during the interview depending on the involvement and comfort felt by the participants. Some work best "eyeball to eyeball," whereas other helpees are threatened by close physical proximity. They need the "safety" of a few feet of space. Although these are comparatively trivial considerations, the helper needs to perceive the implications of the setting for accomplishing the goals of the interview.

Opening. Opening the interview sometimes presents problems. Assuming that the helpee initiates the process, a relaxed expectant attitude on the helper's part usually enables him to state his reasons for coming or what he feels at the moment. If he has difficulty expressing himself, simple leads are helpful, such as "Please tell me what's on your mind," "What did you wish to discuss with me?", "I'm interested in knowing where you're at; please fill me in." Note that the lead is vague so as to allow him to pick it up any way he wishes. Do not imply that he has a "problem" or that he has come into some kind of clinical setting where he is expected to act in a certain way. In less formal kinds of helping situations, even more natural conversational openers would be effective. When the helper has initiated the interview, an honest opening statement regarding why he asked the helpee to come is appropriate.

STAGE 2: CLARIFICATION

The goals of this stage are to clarify the helpee's statements of why he wants help and to get a better feel for how the helpee sees his problem and general life situation. It is not necessary to assume that all helpees come with defined "problems," a general descriptive term for helpee concern.

Use of questions. It is a common tactical error of helpers at this point to begin asking questions. The helpee often feels interrogated, and as a result, threatened. He may perceive this interview as a problem-solving session, such that if all the facts were brought out, the solutions would be apparent or forthcoming from the wisdom of the helper. Asking questions reinforces the kind of "help set" that physicians model when we describe our symptoms and complaints to them. Physicians usually offer a diagnosis after such elaborate questioning. The history and diagnoses are followed with suggestions and prescriptions. Our goal in psychological help is to discourage the above passive-receptive set. We do it by resisting the temptation to ask many questions and mainly by listening and reflecting the feelings expressed by the helpee. We try to suspend judgments and to limit diagnostic thinking, especially in the early stages, although as indicated in the experience list of figure 4, the helper is thinking about the experiential world of the helpee and is trying to get into his perceptual framework much of the time. *Diagnosis* is an important step in some kinds of specialized helping with very disturbed people, but within the framework of helping described in this book it has no place.

The helper encourages the helpee to elaborate and clarify his statements about the nature and kind of help he seeks. This process is not belabored, however, because helpees often do not know *why* they want help. Frequently, they are aware only of some behaviors that make them uncomfortable, ineffective, angry, or anxious. Sometimes they are aware only of vague feelings of discomfort. It is not fruitful, therefore, to ask "why" questions, even though this tactic is tempting. It is so easy, for example, to engage in a questioning routine around "Why do you feel this way? Why did you do that? Why don't you try . . . ?" It is more productive to keep the helpee focused on both feeling and cognitive levels by dealing with "what" questions, if such seem necessary to keep him exploring. The following illustrative questions, for example, usually are productive: "What are you feeling right now? What is going on in you? What did you do?"

Another consideration at this opening level of problem statements is to assist the helpee to determine who "owns" the problem. Is the problem his own exclusively, such as feeling depressed? Does the problem involve a relationship owned by the two persons? For example, in a parent-child problem the parent comes for help with his child. He talks mainly about the child, when in reality he owns the problem because he feels the concern. The child does not. A school counselor receives a child referral from a teacher "for help." It becomes apparent that the teacher is the helpee because he or she has the problem, not the child. The implication here for the helper is to be sure who his helpee really is. Is it the person sitting before him, or someone else in that person's life space? Stage 2 goals then, are to make clear who the principal helpee is and to clarify the helpee's reasons for coming or being referred.

STAGE 3: STRUCTURE

As the helpee explains his reasons for seeking help, or the helper explains why he is offering help, the principal question becomes "What are the conditions under which we will work?" The goal for Stage 3 is to decide whether to proceed with the relationship and on what terms. The sequence of questions that must be answered to reach the goal of Stage 3 are listed as follows:

Helper questions

1. Am I able to work with this person (skills, knowledge)?
2. Do I want to work with him (comfort, compatibility)?
3. Can I meet his expectations (given my skills and knowledge)?
4. What kind of structure do we need to proceed (informal understanding, counseling contract, leave the issue open)?
5. What am I expecting of him (time, place, effort, commitment, responsibility)?

Helpee questions

1. Is this a person I can trust?
2. Will he be helpful on my terms?
3. What will his terms be?
4. Will this relationship get me more involved than I want to be?
5. Am I willing to commit myself to a relationship agreement on his terms, or will we work it out together?
6. If I agree to a "contract" to do specific things, can I get out if I want to?

Before a relationship proceeds the questions above must be answered, at least tentatively, by the two parties to the helping relationship.

Stage 3 structures vary considerably in complexity and formality; however, most helping relationships in life take place at a very *ad hoc,* informal level where either person may withdraw easily at any time. Neither person has a very firm commitment to the other, much like casual friendships. Persons manning crisis center phones and interviews, for example, do not quibble about the niceties of relationship building. They work with the person in crisis where he is now. Questions such as the above are worked out later if a relationship is indicated. Helpers who take their work seriously feel the need for more commitment and structure, yet they want to maintain a close informal relationship with the helpee. Most helpers, therefore, engage in a process called *struc-turing.*

Structuring procedure.   Structuring defines the nature, limits, and goals of the prospective helping relationship. During this process the roles, responsibilities, and possible commitments of both helpee and helper are outlined. The helper generally indicates the steps to reach the helpee's goals so that he has a clearer idea of where he is going and about how long it will take to get there. This does not mean that the process is planned and that it is precisely predictable, but there are enough general principles and fairly predictable stages for helping relationships to give the helpee a rough idea. The helpee should know where he is (type of agency and type of help offered), who the helper is (qualifications, limitations), and why he is there (purpose of the interview). If these are not made clear in the referral process, the agency brochures, or the opening comments of Stage 1, they need to be faced before proceeding.

One view of structuring indicates that structure is implicit and that it evolves naturally, not needing to be discussed formally and obviously. Each helper must develop his own style; and he must be flexible so as to adapt to different helpee circumstances. The main point here is that attention must be paid to the understanding of why this particular helping relationship exists. Lack of such structure may precipitate unnecessary anxiety in the helpee because the relationship is too ambiguous. On the other hand, the helper's anxiety level may be so high that he feels a compulsive need to structure frequently for his own security.

Some of the advantages of agreements on structure are that the *time* to be spent will be clear, both for the first interview and for the total process. Any *fees* involved should be frankly discussed at this stage. *Action limits* are often discussed when an incident takes place.

In working with a young child, for example, it is necessary to point out that he can attack the toys or say anything he wishes, but he cannot attack the people present. *Role limits* are usually discussed in the early stages because roles may be contradictory. One may offer help unconditionally on the one hand, yet he may exercise some kind of judgmental authority over the helpee on the other hand, just because of the reality of the work. An example is the teacher who is often in the position of helper, but who also exercises authority over the students. Many agency workers who administer public programs are in similar positions. Without making a big point of this issue, it is important that these conflicting roles should be made clear to helpees. If the helper is a professional, it is not productive to discuss details about differences and similarities among the helping professions, unless there seems to be some crucial misunderstanding. An example would be perceiving the helper as possessing a medical degree when he does not have such credentials.

Process structure.   An additional element of structuring that takes place usually in Stage 3 is called *process structure.* If help is to proceed efficiently and constructively the helpee must accept responsibility for his share of the interview, and he must know how to express himself in a manner that allows the helper to be maximally helpful. Examples of such process values and norms are that present feelings are important data to bring out, that talking about one's self freely and honestly here is expected and accepted, that taking responsibility for any choices and actions is necessary, and that although the interview may start on a vague and ragged note, things become more specific and clear as the interview progresses. Much of this process structure comes out naturally from events in the interview and much comes from effective modeling of these behaviors by the helper. The exact form of these process norms depends largely on the theoretical view of the helping process held by the helper, again a reason for considering seriously one's theory of the helping process. The nature and timing of structuring is a controversial issue among helpers. The range of possible views has been presented here so you can experiment and develop the style most effective for you.

Formal contracts.   Helpers who are inclined toward a more behavioral approach to the helping process speak of a formal event in Stage 3, called the *contract.* This is an agreement between the helper and helpee that they will work toward certain *goals,* that each will carry out specific *responsibilities* to achieve the goals, and that certain specific *outcomes* will be taken as evidence that the help was successful. An example is the helpee who sees his problem as one of making a career

change. He agrees to seek certain kinds of information, to keep a log of his homework on planning, and to consider the helping process successful when he arrives at three options for choice with confirming and limiting data for each choice. In a more interpersonal type of problem area, such as excessive shyness, the helpee may agree to spend about 10 hours with the helper and follow a prescribed set of exercises possibly involving relaxation methods, trying assertive social behaviors, and agreeing to make two new acquaintances each week. The helping interviews then are devoted to discussing the helpee's feelings about the homework tryouts, learning new skills, revising goals, and looking at evidence of progress. Chapter 8 includes more detail about contracting.

STAGE 4: RELATIONSHIP

The discussion above on structure and contracts assumes that the decision has been made to give a helping relationship an extended tryout. The goal of Stage 4 is to increase the depth of the relationship and the intensity of helpee commitment. It is understood clearly that either the helper or the helpee may bring up the possibility of terminating the relationship by mutual agreement. Stages 1 through 3 usually take place in the first contact so that the helpee knows when he leaves what will happen next and what is expected of him if the relationship is to continue. During this time also the relationship has been deepening in the manner described under Stage 1, namely increasing trust and openness. The relationship should be firmly established by the end of Stage 4, with the helpee ready to go to work specifically toward goals announced upon his arrival and as clarified and amplified in Stages 2 and 3.

Silence. The function of the pause, or silence, is of concern at all stages; but it is of particular significance in the relationship and exploratory stages. Pauses have many meanings which require different handling. The helpee may stop talking as a *resistive* act because he doesn't feel comfortable about revealing himself further. The trust level may not be sufficiently strong. It is indicated by awkward glancing about, flushing, and abrupt changes of topic. If this hunch turns out to be valid, then further discussion of the relationship between helpee and helper is indicated.

A pause may mean the helpee is temporarily *stopped* in his ongoing exploration. He appears preoccupied with his thoughts and sometimes distressed, mainly because he feels blocked in his desire to go on. He may need some quiet time alone to pull his feelings together before he goes on with his verbal exploration. This is often a very productive time and the most helpful thing to do is to quietly wait until he is ready to go on. Sometimes inner struggles take place during these silent periods which may last several minutes; occasionally the helpee will emerge with a significant insight or expression of feeling.

A pause may mean he has come to the *end of a thought* or discussion unit. Typical tapes of helping interviews are characterized by these natural pauses, much like conversation. The helper and helpee then work out a new topic direction. The helpee, for example, may mention several things on his mind, and the helper responds with silence or attention to one item, thus starting a new topic. The helper's attention has a rewarding effect that encourages the helpee to go exploring that new topic further. The helper may suggest several possibilities from which the helper chooses. Usually this is a natural process with attention by both helper and helpee to the nonverbal cues of the other.

STAGE 5: EXPLORATION

This is the working stage when the helper becomes more active and assertive. Through the first stages he is attempting to understand where the helpee is right now and how he sees his world. This task involves listening, clarifying, and structuring methods. The helpee has been taking the lead. By Stage 5, the helper has a more clear grasp of who the helpee is, what he wants, and how he can be helped. There are two key questions at this exploration stage: What changes in helpee behavior are appropriate and needed to achieve his goals? What strategies for intervention will most likely produce these outcomes? The term *interventions* is used commonly in helping circles to designate the techniques that helpers initiate.

What is done at this stage and beyond is tailored to the kind of problem the helpee brings, whether primarily planning, problem solving, interpersonal conflict, or intrapersonal feeling problems. The methods of intervention described in the following chapters are designed to give the helper a wider spectrum of skills and strategies that he can employ selectively to specific helpee problems and expected outcomes. The specific *process goals* for the helper at this stage, however, are as follows:

1. Maintain and enhance the relationship (trust, ease, safety).
2. Deal with feelings in helper and helpee that interfere with progress toward their goals.
3. Encourage the helpee to explore his problem or feelings further (clarify, amplify, illustrate, specify), so helpee's self-awareness is expanded.

4. Encourage the helpee to clarify and further specify his goals.
5. Gather necessary facts that will contribute to the solution of the helpee's problem.
6. Decide to continue or terminate the relationship.
7. Teach skills required to reach helpee goals (demonstrating, modeling, coaching).
8. Initiate helpee homework activities that move him toward his goals (tryout, evaluation, progress).

In the exploratory stage there is a strong tendency to turn inward while describing feelings and delineating problems. This is expected, but the helpee should understand that exploration of feelings and problems is primarily a prelude to *action* for the consolidation and planning stages. Here he moves outside of himself once again toward putting his expanded awareness and new insights into action plans. It is a phase described by Carkhuff and Berenson (1967) as "emergent directionality."

Sometimes the helpee feels so good after the exploratory stage that he thinks his problems are solved and all is well. Some helpers think this is the time to terminate, and it may well be an appropriate time; but this may merely be a good feeling of relief of tension with no specific behavior change in sight. This condition is a critical point in a helping relationship.

Another critical point in the exploratory stage is when the helper is involved in extensive exploration of his feelings and he experiences discouragement. He may want to terminate out of sheer exhaustion and disillusionment with the process. At this point discussion of his feelings of the moment is appropriate, followed by several options: (1) reduce the intensity of exploration by moving to another topic; (2) continue exploring feelings in greater depth; (3) terminate exploration with this helper and consider rebuilding a relationship with another. The third option is especially appropriate when the helper's discomfort with intensive feelings becomes apparent.

Another issue is how assertive the helper should be. In the early stages the helper usually is fairly unassertive, and he encourages the helpee to explore on his own initiative. Helpee responsibility for the direction and content of the interview is emphasized by helpers of all theoretical views and styles. Helpers tend to become more active, however, as the process lengthens. As the process moves closer to the planning and action stages, the helper becomes an active partner bringing all his helping skills to bear.

Transference and countertransference feelings. As a result of increasing intensity of interaction the helpee experiences specific feelings toward the helper that he may have felt only vaguely in the early stages. These feelings range widely from admiring and affectionate types to angry and rejecting feelings. Some reactions may be due to specific behaviors of the helper, but it is more likely that a condition called *transference* is taking place. This is a common event in all human relationships where feelings once felt toward someone close to us are now projected to the immediate helper. Examples are feelings about a parent carried over from childhood. One may see his father symbolically in the helper who now has a position of some authority and power over him. He responds to the helper in the same way he responded to his father in earlier years.

We are unaware, of course, that transference is a likely explanation for our feelings. Unless this phenomenon is understood, and discussed if necessary, much effort is expended that is not related to the problem at hand. It may be possible that a frank discussion of authority problems growing out of the present relationship between the helper and helpee could become a growth experience; this is a matter of helper judgment and specific goals for the particular relationship. When discussing a planning problem with a helpee, for example, it would be inappropriate to spend the limited time talking about transference feelings. It is important to realize, however, that they exist.

A similar condition takes place in the helper who may see the helpee as an ungrateful child, for example. He too may be unaware of the source of his own feelings of annoyance or discomfort with this helpee. He may get sleepy, have difficulty attending, tighten up, sympathize with the helpee, or become argumentative, for example. In the helper these are known as *countertransference* feelings with the same explanation as above for transference.

The important question is not whether countertransference occurs, but what can the helper do about it? If he views these behaviors as signals of unresolved difficulties in his own life, he can take care of the matter by discussing this possibility briefly with the helpee, so he knows at least that the problem resides more in the helper than in their relationship. This should help to resolve some emotional difficulties in the present relationship. For the long term, however, the helper should think about a personal growth experience for himself to expand his own awareness, and hopefully, to change his behavior. Discussing the matter with colleagues is one "first aid" kind of maneuver. Studying video tapes of his work with the help of a colleague, and reflecting on what he sees there, is another. Finally, some kind of personal counseling or encounter group experience, where the helper can explore his feelings, obtain feedback on his behavior, and try out new forms of responding, may be an answer.

Helping, especially in its more formal aspects of counseling and psychotherapy, is a powerful interpersonal influence process. Strong

(1968) studied this process and found that helpers who present themselves so as to be perceived as experts, attractive and trustworthy, are much more influential with helpees than those who are not so perceived. Effective helpers do indeed have power and influence. One consequence is that helpees react to them with a variety of feelings. Helpers, similarly, react in a variety of ways when helpees treat them as influential experts. You, as a helper must be aware of your style of response on this issue.

STAGE 6: CONSOLIDATION

Whereas the bulk of the helping time usually is spent in the work of Stage 5, the task of settling on alternative choices and plans or of practicing the new skills is an important part of the helping process. That inevitable point comes where the helpee must *decide* or *act* and stop talking about himself, his problems, or his possible plans. This consolidation stage flows from the exploratory and blends into the planning stage to follow, but its distinctive process goals are to further clarify feelings, pin down alternative actions, and practice new skills.

Occasionally helpees are so committed to their tasks and have been through the exploratory stages so many times before that they move quickly to the consolidation and planning stages. In such cases, the bulk of the time is spent in decision-making and planning. This brief description of the consolidation, planning and action stages compared to the more elaborate explanation of issues at earlier stages in no way diminishes their importance or time priority.

STAGE 7: PLANNING

This stage is characterized by rational planning processes where plans for termination and continuing alone are formulated. The process goals for this stage are to crystallize discussions of earlier stages into a specific plan of action and to decide that growth has proceeded to the point where termination of the relationship is indicated. Any tag ends of feelings are worked through, and bringing up new topics with feelings is discouraged. In helping processes that are heavily cognitive, such as career-type planning interviews, this stage becomes quite lengthy since many action steps to accomplish the plan need to be formulated. For example, schools need to be contacted and application papers completed.

Discussions of stages 6 and 7 have been comparatively brief since the strategies and methods most used in these stages are presented in chapters 6 through 8.

STAGE 8: TERMINATION

In this stage the accomplishments are summarized. Usually a general evaluation of what was accomplished in light of the goals takes place. If the goals were not achieved, this fact is discussed in terms of hypotheses as to why they were not realized.

There are many methods of terminating a relationship, and each helper must develop his own. Summarizing the process as indicated above is one effective method. A helpful procedure is to ask the helpee to summarize. If a number of plans were made or steps decided, a written summary developed jointly will help. Keeping the conversation at an intellectual level tends to discourage further exploration of feeling. If the process has involved several interviews, then *spreading* the last couple of contacts overtime will tend to de-escalate the involvement. Reference to the agreed *time limits* along with the summary facilitates termination. *Referral* may be indicated if the helpee feels a sense of incompleteness and the helper is reluctant to continue the relationship. Leaving the door open for possible *follow-ups* may make the termination less abrupt. Frequently in agencies like schools, the helper may want to maintain a kind of *standby* relationship to observe and occasionally facilitate the helpee's further development.

Leave-taking is not the problem that is usually anticipated if the stages discussed above have unfolded satisfactorily. There is a natural awareness that "this is the end." The helpee is eager to leave since he usually feels good about his new autonomy and problem solutions. Occasionally he even harbors some feelings of resentment (usually projected to the helper) that he needed help in the first place. Feelings of gratitude are expressed sometimes, but the helper should be wary of these since the goal was to have the helpee feel that he solved his own problem and that he really did not need the help after all. To have grateful helpees, though, expands the self-esteem of the helper. Sometimes helpees have lingering dependency feelings expressed as reluctance to leave. They bring up "just one more thing" or prolong the goodbye ceremony excessively. Some helpees literally need to be led out the door.

In this chapter on the helping process a wide range of issues were discussed. Such a chapter presents a dilemma. On the one extreme are those helpers who say the helping process evolves. You do what comes naturally as in developing a friendship; you trust your feelings since there are no specific cognitive guidelines. At the other extreme are those helpers who view the process as a highly structured enterprise that can be described in terms of precise objectives, steps, methodologies, and outcomes. A middle position was presented here that incorporates elements from diverse theoretical views about the helping process within the context of everyday practical considerations.

Outcomes you should expect from studying this chapter

You can: (1) list seven dimensions of a helping relationship; (2) describe and illustrate the general sequence of events in the helping process as the helper and helpee experience these events; (3) identify eight stages in the helping process from entry to termination and cite examples of typical issues that must be faced at each stage. The principal outcome expected is that you have begun to develop your own "cognitive map" of the helping process which is useful to you in facing the numerous issues of facilitating a helping relationship. The final test of your mastery of this chapter is your capacity to demonstrate your ability to initiate, maintain, and terminate a helping relationship that leads to specific helpee goals.

Suggestions for further study

BRAMMER, L., and SHOSTROM, E. *Therapeutic Psychology: Fundamentals of Actualization Counseling and Psychotherapy.* Englewood Cliffs, N.J.: Prentice-Hall, 1968. (Ch. 4 on steps and critical points in the counseling process.)

CARKHUFF, R., and BERENSON, B. *Beyond Counseling and Psychotherapy.* New York: Holt, Rinehart & Winston, 1967. (A model of the counseling process based on facilitative process.)

CORLISS, R., and RABE, P. *Psychotherapy from the Center: A Humanistic View of Change and Growth.* Scranton, Pa.: International Textbook, 1969. (A humanistic view of the process, especially Ch. 2 on starting, Ch. 5 on growth, Ch. 6 on termination.)

KRUMBOLTZ, J., and THORESON, C. *Behavioral Counseling: Cases and Techniques.* New York: Holt, Rinehart & Winston, 1969. (A collection of articles on the helping process from a behavioral viewpoint.)

MARTIN, D. *Learning-based Client-centered Therapy.* Monterey, Calif.: Brooks-Cole, 1972. (An approach to the helping process based on a blend of behavioral and client-centered views.)

TRUAX, C., and CARKHUFF, R. *Toward Effective Counseling and Psychotherapy.* Chicago: Aldine, 1967. (A critique of the helping process on the basis of research findings and practice. Also, an analysis of the effective ingredients in psychotherapy.)

5 | Learning how to learn basic helping skills

The purposes of this chapter are to describe various methods for learning helping skills and to provide a framework for detailed study of each skill cluster. The term "skills cluster" refers to groups of related helping skills. Labels used for the clusters have fairly common meaning among persons in the helping professions, but there is no standard terminology or classification. As a result, each teacher has his own special way of classifying helping skills. You must select the skills and sequences for applying those skills that suit your style best.

To complicate the learning task further, each student of helping skills has his own best learning style. Some, for example, learn skills best by seeing a demonstration or a model film of the skill; others want to read about the skill and understand the rationale and steps before practicing it. Some want to try the skill in simulated, hence less risky, experiences. Still others learn most effectively by experiencing a helping relationship with little preparation; then he sees a video tape and receives feedback on his performance. This is known as the experiential approach.

There are three basic strategies for learning helping skills general principles—skills practice, experiential, and didactic knowledge. These differences in teaching-learning style are the reason for taking space here to talk about learning how to learn. Knowing these styles will enhance your awareness of various helping skills and your understanding of the remaining chapters, but just reading about them probably will not improve your skills much. You need practice under the strategy best suited to you, and then you need feedback on your performance of the helping skills.

Outcomes that you can expect as a result of studying this chapter are competencies to (1) identify a style of learning best suited to you; (2) list twenty theoretical concepts and vocabulary terms from varied theories used to describe helping skills; (3) list twelve basic skill clusters in the realms of understanding, comfort, crisis utilization, and action; and (4) describe four methods for learning helping skills.

Part and whole approaches

MICROSKILLS METHODS

The skills presented in the remaining chapters have been demonstrated to be effective through research or practice. The basic method for learning these precise skills is called microskills training. This is an instructional strategy that divides a large category of skills into simple teachable behavioral components. These skills then can be combined into numerous interview combinations.

An advantage of the microskills approach is that the instructor can be much more specific about describing helping skills, rather than using general suggestions such as "Listen to your helpees!" The next chapter will describe the component skills of listening, for example, and how they can be learned. The microskills are so basic to effective communication that they fit easily into every theoretical framework or helper setting. Effective helpers use these skills, not as mechanically applied formulas for helping, but as a repertoire of basic communication skills.

It is paradoxical that the main limitation of the microskills approach is its specificity. Integrating the components into a smooth helping process is not easy. It is like teaching swimming by training the person to use his arms, hands, legs, and breathing apparatus separately—and then telling him "Now you are a swimmer." How can he learn the component skills and then combine them into the beautifully coordinated act we call swimming? This is the problem in learning complex helping skills also. It seems artificial to be so analytical, but experience in counselor education shows that students can become so involved in skills practice that they perceived them not as techniques but as natural manifestations of good human relations and effective interpersonal communications.

A microskills approach provides you with considerable flexibility of choice, since you have many options from which to choose. The microskills teaching approach seems the best compromise between a strategy of teaching general principles, which assumes transfer of those principles to skills, and the precise "cookbook" approach that attempts to tell you what to do and how to do it under specific circumstances. It is important to maintain a broad perspective on the whole helping process (the polished swimmer, remember?), as well as attend to the fundamental skills. The challenge is to produce a smoothly integrated champion from careful attention to fundamentals without making those fundamentals the exclusive focus.

Chapter 1 stressed the importance of fundamental component skills training, combined with helper self-understanding and broad awareness of the total helping task, as the most effective preparation for the helping function. Seeing appropriate and inappropriate models, along with understanding the ideas and purposes behind the skill, makes the learning process even more effective. Practicing the skill and receiving feedback on the tryout performances are essential elements also. Then, repeating performances until the desired level of skill is achieved constitutes the final phase of this model.

Ivey (1972) used a training model in his study of microcounseling, for example, that contained the following steps: (1) a five-minute taped interview to establish a natural baseline measure of the trainees' interviewing behavior; (2) reading a description of the technique; (3) viewing video tape models of effective and ineffective use of skills; (4) viewing his initial baseline tape noting specific instances of using the new skill effectively and ineffectively; (5) discussing the skill procedures with a supervisor or colleague; (6) completing another five-minute taped interview sample with the same helpee, thus giving the trainee an opportunity to demonstrate his skill; (7) repeating the cycle until the desired level of competence is achieved. The success of this method hinges on the adequacy of the supervisory relationship to a large extent. This is one reason that it is difficult to learn helping skills by independent study alone.

The key to improvement in the microcounseling skills approach is immediate feedback on performance. The new skill is practiced until the desired performance standard is met. Truax and Carkhuff (1967) utilized a similar program integrating the teaching of concepts and experiencing feedback on actual performance of basic skills. Gordon (1970) developed a skills package designed for small groups of parents or teachers who want to practice more effective ways of communicating with children. Kagan (1971) has packaged a program on "influencing human interaction" which has filmed models, skill practice units, and feedback systems called "interpersonal process recall." This is a method of video taping a short interview with a helpee. An independent interviewer talks with the helpee immediately afterward about his reactions to the experience while the helper watches the inquiry interview. Then the helper is interviewed similarly. Finally, both come together with the person conducting the inquiry interviews and the observers to discuss their reactions to the original helping interview and to make recommendations for improvement of skills and process.

Others who have published experimental programs involving media, readings, and exercises in basic human interaction skills are Danish (1971), Kagan (1971), Jung (1971), and Cunningham (1970). The last mentioned item is an example of a packaged program for increasing competencies of practicing counselors. Appendix A of this book includes samples of brief skills practice exercise guides that the author has used in training programs.

The programs cited above are examples of bridging the gap between theory and practice. They are not established do-it-yourself programs but experimental systems designed to help groups master basic human interaction skills with a minimum of expert instructional leadership.

Simulations. The best known example of this learning strategy, related to microcounseling, is role playing. The trainee takes the role of a helpee and tries to become that person as much as possible. Although the actual problem is artificial, the simulated helpee tries to make it as real as possible, even to taking a problem from his own experience. The helper then simulates the helper role, continuing for about ten minutes, or until enough time has passed for adequate practice of the basic skill. This can be done as a demonstration and discussion stimulator in front of a group or in helping trios to be described in the next section.

A variation on the role playing method is to ask three persons to leave the room while the group develops a helpee role and asks one of the group to simulate the helpee. Then the absent "helpers" are brought in one at a time to do their helping sequences with the simulated helpee. One advantage of this method is that the group has several styles of helping to compare, and the feedback from the simulated "helpee" to the interviewers is most often a powerful educational experience for all. This can be extended into more complex dramatic situations where classrooms, families, and meetings are simulated and acted out with props, scenes, and directors. An advanced form of this type of simulation is known as "psychodrama."

Occasionally coached helpees or even professional actors have been utilized to provide simulated helping conditions close to real problems.

Kagan (1971) has used video taped actors presenting different human problems in short clips. The helper trainee is then asked to make a response as if this were an interview. He imagines he is alone with the person on the screen.

A useful teaching method for basic skills is the "round robin helping trio." Here three people who are learning the skills together practice and give each other feedback on their performance. One is a simulated helpee, another the helper, and the third an observer of the process. After a brief skills practice sequence they stop and discuss the experience, including the observer's comments. Then, the whole process is repeated two more times with trio members changing roles, hence the "round robin" label. This process is illustrated in figure 5.

FIGURE 5.   Round robin helping trio.

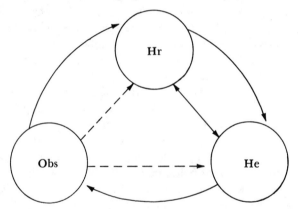

A whole array of "games" has been constructed to deal with real life problems in simulated form. There are "career," "war," "ghetto," and "marriage" games. These games allow intense involvement without the risks and complexities of real life situations. At the same time they provide sufficient data when properly conducted to generate very productive learnings about self and interpersonal relationships. Although they are not direct helping simulation devices, they provide awareness for the helper on how he reacts in conflict, prejudice, crisis, problem-solving, and decision-making settings.

EXPERIENTIAL LEARNING

Beginning with a real experience is the key feature. Experiential learning involves doing the actual task and then discussing the experience and learning derived. It is known as the "do-look-learn" approach.

The helper, for example, actually interviews a person seeking help; then the helper and helpee describe how they felt about the experience and what they did. The observers, if there are some, offer their emotional and cognitive reactions. Then, the principals and the observer group discuss what they *learned* from the experience—about helping skills, communication skills, or listening methods.

The values of this kind of experiential learning are very great, but it has some limitations. It is a high risk activity for the helper because he takes the great leap into the experience without knowing the consequences. Sometimes he ends the experience in a heap of frustration and humiliation, or at worst, with no feelings. Occasionally he feels the exhilaration flowing from discovery of new resources and skills not hitherto realized. Such learning has some risks for the helpee too, because the helping encounter usually is not a simulated situation but a real plea for help. There is an ethical question about assigning a naive student helper to a helpee struggling with real problems. In formal training settings this issue is resolved somewhat by the usual presence of an experienced supervisor and fellow trainees who provide support as well as critical feedback on training performance.

Various growth groups designed to provide helper trainees with self-awareness and skills practice fall in this experiential learning category. Here, the trainees arrange themselves in a group and interact at increasingly more trusting and close interpersonal levels. Learning outcomes flow from the frequent efforts of the leader, or learning facilitator, to stop the action and to look at both the learning process they are going through and what is happening to them as individuals. During the group process itself, however, members are constantly giving and receiving feedback (honest reactions) to their helping skills. Some instructors of basic helping skills lean almost entirely on this experiential form of learning through groups to provide the kind of self-awareness and skills training required of helpers.

A variation on experiential learning common among early helping professionals was the "didactic analysis." This method of learning the form of therapy known as psychoanalysis by going through an analysis experience oneself is still utilized. Counselors and psychotherapists often learn the principles and skills of the helping process in a similar manner, but the principal limitation of this method is its costs. It is literally a one-to-one tutorial method of skill learning.

The traditional didactic strategy of teaching general principles and knowledge has little efficacy when used alone. When combined with skills training and experiential learning, however, behavioral science fact and theory have their place in a helper program. They provide a basis for judgment and framework for organizing experiences, such as the case made for theory in chapter 3.

A combined strategy approach

The learning system I prefer, and that I see as having much support in research and practice, combines the microskills, experiential learning, and didactic strategies. My approach is roughly as follows: (1) practice microskills in a simulated laboratory setting with constant critiques; (2) expose oneself to intensive self-awareness experiences (usually along with 1); (3) practice putting skills together into appropriate patterns in a practicum setting with real helpees and close supervision; (4) practice skills in natural helping relationships in agencies, at home, and with friends. Special knowledge and skill inputs such as theory, research methods, and referral resources are acquired as needed through conventional classes, independent study, or tutorials.

With the current emphasis on experiential learning there appears to be growing skepticism about the value of direct teaching of helper characteristics, such as sensitivity to feelings of helpees. The old assumptions about automatic transfer from lectures on "how to do it" to actual practice are not valid, but forms of programmed instruction may be useful as supplements to other methods. Bullmer (1972), for example, studied the acquisition of interpersonal perceptual skill through a programmed self-instructional method. He demonstrated that effective person perceivers can be "made" through knowledge of conconcepts related to interpersonal perception, sources of error in perception, identifying feelings, and identifying hidden meaning. The learner then practices applying this knowledge through examples. The basic issue, again, is how can you as a learner make the best use of the three basic strategy principles—experiential, skills training, and didactic knowledge?

In summary, it is essential to have practice in basic skills (through exercises and simulations), opportunities for self-awareness (through counseling and group experience), and exposure to real life problems and helping relationships to put the whole process together. While it appears to be a safe assumption that some of the learnings acquired in laboratory settings and independent reading transfer to helping relationships, there is no substitute for direct experience with immediate feedback on performance.

Basic theory underlying skills application

Before introducing the skills chapters, it may be useful to summarize the basic theoretical views underlying those skills. There are four theoretical threads running through the skills to be described and illustrated in the remaining chapters, and concepts from all four types of theories will be drawn upon.

NEEDS

The first is the *need approach* to motivation described in chapter 1. Human beings are energized by basic psychological and physiological needs that push for satisfaction and stabilization of the personality, but occasionally they seek risky behavior to provide variety. That people act to satisfy their needs is the basic idea of this viewpoint. Helping skills are designed to assist the helpee to fulfill his needs for understanding, comfort, and action.

LEARNING

A second thread helping to tie the helping skills together is a behavior change, or learning, approach. The key concepts useful for skill development are those already described in chapter 3, such as *modeling.* Modeling is the use of examples of effective and ineffective helping skills. *Reinforcement* is another key learning concept that is stated simply as management of rewards. Behaviors that are rewarded tend to become fixed in the repertoire of the person. Satisfying a need tends to be a reinforcing condition, for example. Conversely, behaviors that are not rewarded, such as those which are ignored or which may even be aversive or noxious, tend to disappear from the behavioral repertoire of the person. The principle of *transfer* is important for skill learning also since skills learned in simulated, or artificial gaming, kinds of settings are transferred to similar real life helping situations. Practicing listening skills in a controlled laboratory setting, for example, can then be applied in comparable helping interviews. *Stimulus substitution,* or reconditioning, also takes place in some kinds of helping situations. We may wish to substitute a relaxation response, for example, for a tension response in a test situation. *Goal setting* and *problem solving* are important in the learning approach also.

AWARENESS

A third theoretical thread covers the idea of *awareness of feelings* and their effects. As indicated in chapter 3, our reality is what we perceive it to be. Therefore, when we talk about understanding, we mean perceiving the helpee's unique way of looking at the world. The helper responds to him in such a way that the helpee perceives himself as being understood. The helpee manifests this understanding by verbal behavior that describes his subjective feelings, such as "I feel confident," or "I feel angry toward you," or "I feel good about you and me," or "Now I know where it's at."

COMMUNICATIONS

A fourth thread that ties the whole skill bundle together is *communications* theory. An underlying assumption in helping is that people do not understand one another because they cannot communicate with one another. Therefore, the skills to be covered in the following chapters are aimed at facilitating interpersonal communication by listening and speaking more clearly. The basic communications problem is to make one's intent as a speaker clear by matching his intent with his words. The result is directness and clarity of meaning.

The usual state of affairs, however, is a communications gap where the effect on the hearer does not match the message the speaker intended, and so, much time is spent in clearing up the resulting misunderstanding. Sometimes this condition is caused by the double message, the one given by one's body, which says "I'm afraid," and one's words, which say "I'm calm and confident." The result is confusion in the hearer and projection of his own meanings on the mixed message.

It seems almost absurdly simple to state that often the most helpful thing we can do is to make it possible for the helpee to improve his communication. This approach includes attention to nonverbal, or body, language as well as speech. Our actions, rather than our words, are more honest and direct forms of communication because we have learned that words can conceal, distort, and deny real feelings, but our bodies do not do so. As one helper, Perls, expressed it clearly, "Our bodies do not lie." One means to make our messages more clear, then, is to get in touch with our bodies (our feelings) so we know what they are saying. By pointing out discrepancies between verbal messages and body messages in helpees, we help them to communicate more consistently and clearly with themself and others.

The preceding discussion implied that communications problems in helping interviews result from unclear intent or confused messages from helpees. One needs to remind himself constantly that communication, being the two-way street that it is, requires that he look into the ways he distorts what he hears from helpees. Are my needs, of which I am unaware, acting as "filters" through which I hear the helpee's message my way? If I am vaguely aware, or creating fantasies about this helpee, do I hear what I *want* to hear? Am I fearful that I will be attacked, seduced, or "conned"? Am I fearful that I might do the same to the helpee? The kinds of awareness and conditions discussed in the preceding chapter under transference and countertransference should help here. The next chapter on understanding skills will go into methods for discovering and managing feelings. The main point here is that unrecognized needs and feelings distort messages and really compound problems enormously.

Classification of skills

There is no standard classification of helping skills or common vocabulary. All helping styles include, however, skills that facilitate expression, awareness, or understanding of feelings, and those that facilitate rational problem solving, decision making, and acting. As we saw in chapter 3, helpers differ in their degree of emphasis on management of internal states or management of the environment as the principal route to behavior change.

Figure 6 contains a classification of skills. The three categories of understanding, support, and action reflect the main helping process goals that are translations of what helpees usually want. These three categories are overlapping in the sense that methods for promoting understanding also provide support and facilitate action.

The chapters that follow will present the basic helping skills to include outcome behaviors expected in the helpee. Although there is little research on the relationship between helper behavior and consequent helpee behavior, there is a body of experience and a set of hypotheses about the connections from which to draw. Steps in the format for the last three chapters on skills are: (1) *what* the skill is; (2) *purposes* for using it; (3) *illustrations* of its use; (4) *outcomes expected* for the helpee; (5) *summary* of guidelines for using the skill.

Outcomes you should expect from studying this chapter

Now you can: (1) identify a style of skill learning best suited to you; (2) plan next steps for improving your helping skills; (3) select a learning method to develop your skills; (4) describe your learning tasks and outcomes with concepts and vocabulary from various theories of

FIGURE 6. Helping skills.

For understanding	For comfort and crisis utilization	For positive action

1. Listening
  1.1 Attending
  1.2 Paraphrasing
  1.3 Clarifying
  1.4 Perception checking
 	
2. Leading
  2.1 Indirect leading
  2.2 Direct leading
  2.3 Focusing
  2.4 Questioning
 	
3. Reflecting
  3.1 Feeling
  3.2 Content
  3.3 Experience
 	
4. Summarizing
  4.1 Feeling
  4.2 Content
  4.3 Process
 	
5. Confronting
  5.1 Describing feelings
  5.2 Expressing feelings
  5.3 Feeding back
  5.4 Meditating
  5.5 Repeating
  5.6 Associating
 	
6. Interpreting
  6.1 Explaining
  6.2 Questioning
  6.3 Fantasizing
 	
7. Informing
  7.1 Giving information
  7.2 Giving advice
  7.3 Suggesting
	1. Supporting
	  1.1 Contacting
	  1.2 Reasuring
	  1.3 Relaxing
	
	2. Crisis intervening
	  2.1 Building hope
	  2.2 Consoling
	  2.3 Controlling
	
	3. Centering
	  3.1 Identifying strengths
	  3.2 Reviewing growth experiences
	  3.3 Recalling peak experiences
	
	4. Referring
		1. Problem solving and decision making
		  1.1 Identifying problems
		  1.2 Changing problems to goals
		  1.3 Analyzing problems
		  1.4 Exploring alternatives and implications
		  1.5 Planning a course of action
		  1.6 Generalizing to new problems
		
		2. Behavior modifying
		  2.1 Modeling
		  2.2 Rewarding
		  2.3 Extinguishing
		  2.4 Desensitizing

helping; and (5) list twelve basic skill clusters in the areas of understanding, comfort and crisis utilization, and action. The following suggested readings contain more detailed information for further work on the expected outcomes for this chapter.

Suggestions for further study

BIGGE, M. *Learning Theory for Teachers.* New York: Harper & Row, 1964. (An elementary description of the principal theories of learning.)

BILODEAU, E., ed. *Principles of Skill Acquisition.* New York: Academic Press, 1969. (A collection of papers on skills from a systems viewpoint.)

BOOCOCK, S., ed. *Simulation Games in Learning.* Beverly Hills, Calif.: Sage Publications, 1968. (A manual on the theory and practice of games as learning aids.)

BRADFORD, L., BENNE, K., and GIBB, J. *T-Group Theory and Laboratory Method.* New York: Wiley, 1964. (An elaboration of the laboratory method and use of T-groups.)

BROWN, G. *Human Teaching for Human Learning.* New York: Viking Press, 1971. (An introduction to confluent education—the integration of cognitive and affective education.)

BRUNER, J. *Toward a Theory of Instruction.* Cambridge, Mass.: Belknap Press, 1966. (How to use research knowledge in forming one's views of the learning process.)

BUGELSKI, B. *The Psychology of Learning Applied to Teaching.* Indianapolis: Bobbs-Merrill, 1971. (How to develop a theory and strategy of learning and instruction.)

CARLSON, E. *Learning through Games: A New Approach to Problem Solving.* Washington, D.C.: Public Affairs Press, 1969. (Learning to solve problems through simulated situations.)

CHESTER, M. *Role Playing Methods in the Classroom.* Chicago: Science Research Associates, 1966. (An introductory approach to role playing teaching methods.)

IVEY, A. *Microcounseling: Interviewing Skills Manual.* Springfield, Ill.: C. C Thomas, 1972. (Suggestions and illustrations for learning micro-counseling skills.)

ROGERS, C. *Freedom to Learn.* Columbus, Ohio: C. E. Merrill, 1969. (An elaboration on experiential learning.)

ZUCKERMAN, D., and HORN, R. *The Guide to Simulation Games for Education and Training.* Cambridge: Information Resources, 1970. (A practical list of games both experimental and marketed.)

6 | *Helping skills for understanding*

This chapter will focus on techniques that promote understanding of self and others. The outcomes you can expect from studying this chapter are competencies to: (1) identify seven helping skills that contribute to helpee self-understanding; (2) cite subskills and give examples from helping interviews; and (3) with practice, use effectively seven basic skill clusters in helping relationships.

The final criterion of success will be your demonstrated performance of the skills such that the helpee feels understood and confirms this feeling with appropriate verbal or nonverbal behavior. You may expect helpees to respond positively to you when they feel you understand them. You can expect that they will talk about themselves and you more freely. They will share their new understandings with you. Later, you may expect helpees to try to change themselves or their circumstances on the basis of their new understandings, skills, and changed environments.

Skill cluster 1: Listening skills

At first glance the term "listening" implies a passive act of taking in the content of the helpee's communication, but actually it involves a very active process of responding to total messages. It includes not only listening with the ears to his words and with the eyes to his body language, but a total kind of perceptiveness which is best described by Reik's (1948) term "listening with the third ear." It means also that we are silent much of the time and that the helpees talk. When the helper can answer in considerable detail the question, "What is going on in this person right now and in his life space?" he is listening with all his perceptual capacities. Listening skills are basic to all interviewing whether the purpose be for gaining information, conducting structured depth interviews, or open informal helping.

ATTENDING

Attending has several subcomponents, which have been studied intensively by Ivey and others (1968). The first of these is *contact*, principally through the eye. The helper attends to the helpee by looking at him, usually at his eyes. It is a way of indicating intense interest in the other person because eyes are one of our key vehicles for communicating. This does not mean that eye contact must be a fixed stare to be effective. If the helper is honestly interested and at ease himself, he will look naturally at the helpee while he is talking. Simply writing about eye contact does not do justice to the power of the eyes to communicate caring and understanding as well as to maintain attention. Think of your own experience when someone looked at you intensively. Sometimes it was done in a vacuous sort of way just to hold your attention. At other times they said with their eyes in a warm way, "Look at me; I hear you; I understand," so that you felt they really cared about you and understood how you were feeling.

Distance between helper and helpee needs experimentation before the most comfortable distance for the two is discovered. Some helpees are very uncomfortable, for example, if the eye contact is less than three feet or so, because they are so socially conditioned against close contact. Helpee nonverbal behavior should be watched for signs of stress or discomfort.

A second element of attending is *posture*. This is usually a natural helper response to interest. Usually he leans toward the helpee in a relaxed manner. Relaxation is important because tenseness tends to take his focus from the helpee to himself, in addition to provoking an empathic tension response in the helpee.

A third related element of attending is *gesture*. The helper communicates much with his body movements. If he flails wildly with his hands, or if he crosses them over his chest in a rather pontifical manner, he will very likely communicate some unintended messages. The purpose for mentioning this obvious fact is to help you be more aware of the messages you send to helpees with gestures. Are the messages ones you intend to communicate?

A fourth attending component is *verbal* behavior. The key characteristic of this component is that it relates to what the helpee has said. The helper does not ask questions, take the topic in a new direction, nor add to the helpee's meaning. An example would be to mention a word or reflect a phrase, from the statements of the helpee to focus further on an idea. Some confirming, yet not too personal, comment such as, "I see what you mean," or "I can appreciate what you went through," or "That certainly seems to tie things together," often helps to keep him exploring and assures him that you are listening.

Why does attending behavior work so well? It is very rewarding according to studies, and helpees like it. The *effect on the helpee* of attending behavior is to *encourage* him to go on verbalizing his ideas or feelings freely. It has a powerful *reinforcing effect,* in other words. It allows the helpee to explore in his own way and tends to build a sense of responsibility for the interview. This is one difference between helping and conversation. In social interaction there is more give and take of opinions, questions, and feelings. Conversely, *selective inattention* by the helper can serve to discourage further exploration of the topic. For example, the helpee may be on a rambling intellectual description of an historical event. You may think it more productive to have him focus on how he feels now about that event, so you attend when he focuses on feelings and ignore him when he is on a story-telling trip. You can see how *controlling* attending behavior can be. Helpees control helpers, too, by giving them verbalizations that hold their attention, and helpers certainly control helpees by their attending behavior.

If the helper is relaxed, the helpee will tend to be more at ease also. One of the most difficult tasks for the beginning helper is to let the helpee tell his story without profuse questioning and jumping from topic to topic in a tense manner.

Attending behavior, furthermore, is a kind of "fail-safe" method to use when opening an interview because it furthers the goals of helpee self-exploration and minimizes the chances of making destructive interventions. Even if an awkward silence takes place, the helper can acknowledge what has just been stated or refer to some earlier comments.

The following list is a summary of guidelines for effective attending behavior:

1. Establish *contact* through looking at the helpee when he talks.
2. Maintain a *natural relaxed posture* which indicates your interest.
3. Use *natural gestures* which communicate your intended messages.

4. Use *verbal statements* which relate to his statements without interruptions, questions, or new topics.

PARAPHRASING

Paraphrasing is a method of restating the helpee's basic message in similar, but usually fewer, words. The main purpose of paraphrasing for the helper is to test his understanding of what the helpee has said. (It is a practical test of your attending too!) A second purpose is to communicate to the helpee that you are trying to understand his basic message, and if successful, that you have been with him during his verbal explorations. A paraphrase executed to the helpee's satisfaction is one objective definition of understanding.

The helper translates his raw perceptions of what the helpee is saying into more simple, precise, and culturally relevant wording. The helper repeats, or feeds back only the helpee's message, and avoids adding his own ideas. To help in this process the helper should ask himself the following question constantly: "What is this person's basic thinking and feeling message to me?" The helper, at the time of a natural break in the flow of ideas and feelings gives his concise summary of what he has been hearing. Usually the paraphrase has heavy cognitive content, although it includes feelings if these are an important part of the helpee's message. The helper should look for some cue that his paraphrase has been helpful. Examples of paraphrasing are:

He: I really think he is a very nice guy; he's so thoughtful, sensitive, and kind. He calls me a lot. He's fun to go out with.

Hr: You like him very much, then.

He: I do, very much.

He: I just don't understand. One minute she tells me to do this, and the next minute to do that.

Hr: She really confuses you.

He: Yeah, she sure does, and besides . . . .

There are some problems in using paraphrasing and other listening component skills. If the helper is not careful, he develops a highly stylized way of responding which may be annoying to the helpee. He may say repeatedly, for example, "I hear you saying. . . ." Using a paraphrase seems a bit artificial at first until the helper experiences some rewards in the form of encouraging responses from the helpee. After a while it feels like a more natural form of communication than the usual questions, opinions, veiled threats, or bland conversation fillers.

The helpee experiences a feeling of being understood as a consequence of paraphrasing. He also may experience more specific results in the form of a clearer perception of what he said and a sense of direction to rambling statements. He tends to like the helper who uses paraphrases skillfully. The final effect of paraphrased statements is that he feels encouraged to go on. When learning paraphrasing skills in a laboratory setting, the students should practice until the "helpee" indicates that the paraphrase is accurate to his satisfaction in at least two out of three trials. Appendix 2 contains a brief illustrative exercise to learn paraphrasing.

Here is a summary of guidelines for paraphrasing:

1. Listen for the *basic message* of the helpee.
2. *Restate* to the helpee a concise and simple summary of his basic message.
3. Observe a *cue*, or ask for a *response,* from the helpee which confirms or disconfirms the accuracy and helpfulness of the paraphrase for promoting his understanding.

CLARIFYING

Clarifying brings vague material into sharper focus. It goes beyond simple paraphrasing in that the helper makes a *guess* regarding the helpee's *basic message* and offers it to the helpee. He may also ask for clarification when he cannot make sense out of the helpee's responses. The message may have been so vague, the wording so confusing, the reasoning so circuitous, or the style so complex, that it is a strain to try to paraphrase. Following are some examples which might follow after one of those rambling helpee monologues: "I'm confused, let me try to state what I think you were saying, . . ." "I lost you there; I'm not clear how you feel about your job; could you give me a brief repeat and an illustration?" "It seems to me you were trying to focus on something there, but the ideas just seemed to tumble over one another." "I'm not sure I understand; could you tell me more?"

This method has a touch of interpreting or explaining how the helper sees the situation, and this interpreting need is one of the strong temptations to which helpers must not submit in the early stage of the relationship. The clarifying remarks are stated in terms of the helper's feelings of confusion thereby avoiding implications of criticism at this tender stage. After all, the confusion may be due to the helper's inattention rather than confusing helpee statements. The effect of clarifying responses or requests on the helpee should be more clear helpee statements, such as efforts to rephrase, to summarize, or to illustrate.

General guidelines for clarifying are:

1. *Admit confusion* about helpee's meaning.
2. Try a *restatement* or *ask for clarification,* repetition, or illustration.

PERCEPTION CHECKING

Perception checking asks the helpee for verification of your perceptions of what he said, usually over several statements. Ask for feedback about the accuracy of your listening. The reason that perception checking is so effective as a listening skill is that it is a method of giving and receiving feedback on the accuracy of the communication. Assumptions that understanding is taking place are checked out with the helpee. Here again, ordinary social conversation differs from a helping interview. We are conditioned to chatter onward socially, even to deliberately confusing the meaning with inuendo, humor, and metaphor. We rarely check with one another about what we really are trying to say. In helping relationships we reverse this process and put a heavy premium on direct and clear communication aided by frequent perception checks.

Examples of helper perception checks are: "You seem to be very irritated with me; is that right?" "I was wondering if the plan you chose is the one you really want. You expressed some doubt; did I hear correctly?" "I want to check with you what I'm hearing. You said that you love your wife, yet in the last few minutes, you said that you can't stand to be with her. I detected strong contradictory feelings toward her; is that the way it appears to you too?"

The effect on the helpee is a feeling of being understood. Listening, followed by perception checking, is a method of clearing up confusing communications quickly. Perception checking thus serves to correct misperceptions of the helper before they increase to misunderstandings.

In summary, guidelines for perception checking are:

1. *Paraphrase* what you think you heard.
2. Ask for *confirmation* directly from the helpee about the accuracy of your perception of what he said.
3. Allow the helpee to *correct your perception* if it was inaccurate.

Listening is the key skill in this cluster. To use it naturally and effectively, the helper must want very much to understand the helpee, to communicate meaningfully with him, and to relate to him with acceptance and trust. Effective listening requires much confidence in helpees' abilities to solve their own problems and to establish their independent identities.

Skill cluster 2: Leading

The purpose of leading is to invite or encourage the helpee to respond to open communication. Although leading skills are used throughout the helping process, they are useful particularly in the opening stages of a relationship to invite verbal expression. The helper slightly anticipates the helpee's direction of thought as a method for stimulating talk. It is analogous to the football passer who anticipates the receiver's path so that the ball and the receiver arrive at the same point. The helper's interventions thus appear to the helpee appropriate to where he wants to go.

Leading sometimes is described in helping literature as the helper's degree of impact upon, or thinking ahead, of the helpee. All helping skills can be rated on the amount of leading involved in their use, but for purposes of this discussion, leading will mean the more specific act of anticipating where the helpee is going and the act of responding with an appropriately encouraging remark.

More specific objectives of leading are: (1) to encourage the helpee to explore his feelings and to elaborate on those he has discussed already; (2) to allow the helpee freedom to explore in a variety of directions and to respond freely to what is going on; and (3) to encourage the helpee to be active in the process and to retain primary responsibility.

INDIRECT LEADING

The main purposes of indirect leading are to get the helpee started and to keep responsibility on him for keeping the interview going. One common use of this idea is to open an interview. Examples are: "What would you like to talk about?" "Perhaps we could start by your telling me where you're at now." "Please tell me why you are here?" Later interview examples are: "Tell me more about that." "You were saying (pause)." "What do you think that means?" "How did you feel?" "Is there anything more you would like to discuss?" The generality of these leads allows the helpee to project his own ideas and direction into the interview. Sometimes, pausing and looking expectantly at the helpee serves as an indirect lead.

The helpee's response to indirect leads is to realize he has an invitation to tell his story or elaborate on what he has said. This is encouraging to most helpees, because they experience more responsibility for the relationship. To others it is threatening or annoying since they often expect the expert to be more active and to do most of the talking, advising, and questioning.

The following are guidelines for indirect leading:

1. Determine the *purpose* of the lead clearly.
2. Keep the lead *general* and deliberately vague.
3. *Pause* long enough for the helpee to pick up the lead.

DIRECT LEADING

Direct leading is a method of focusing the topic more specifically. This method also encourages the helpee to elaborate, clarify, or illustrate what he has been saying. Sometimes a strong element of suggestion is included. Some examples are: "Tell me more about your mother." "Suppose we explore your ideas about teaching a little more." "How do you mean—funky?" "Can you think of an illustration which happened recently?"

The behavior of the helpee in response to a direct lead usually is to comply with the specifics of the lead, particularly if the helper's attitude manifests interest to match his words. The main longer range consequence, however, is to enhance his awareness and, later understanding through more elaborate exploration of his feelings.

The guidelines for direct leading are:

1. Determine the *purpose* of the lead.
2. Express the *purpose* in words which elicit specific elaboration.
3. Allow the helpee *freedom to follow* your lead.

FOCUSING

Focusing serves to pinpoint the talk on something that the helper thinks would be fruitful to explore. It is used when the helpee is rambling vaguely and seemingly without focus. Often, in the early stages, helpees will wander over numerous topics, sometimes in circular fashion. Occasionally, the helper's indirect leads have encouraged this wandering. If allowed to continue for several minutes it tends to become confusing for both. When the helper thinks that the helpee has explored the main topics of his concern, the helper deliberately focuses on one aspect of the helpee's talk which he feels could be elaborated productively. Sometimes he stops the helpee and asks him to choose an aspect on which to focus since another purpose of focusing is to emphasize a feeling or idea from a vast array of intellectual verbiage. It is also a way of aiding the helpee to get in touch with his feelings.

Some illustrations of focusing leads are: "Please elaborate more specifically on those feelings about your mother." "You have been discussing many topics the last few minutes; could you pick the most important one to you and tell me more about it?" "How would you choose one word to describe the last five minutes talk?" "We have been talking about words, words, words, but I haven't detected much feeling yet; could you name a feeling you have right now?" "What were your feelings as we've been talking?" "Let's not talk for awhile. I suggest you close your eyes and try to get in touch with what you are feeling. . . ."

Focusing can sometimes be done by picking out one word or a short phrase from the helpee's talk and repeating it with a question mark or with emphasis. For example, after he has been talking about how confusing his relationships with his supervisor have been, you might say, "Confusing?" The effect is, "Tell me more!" The one word focusing method can be effective in keeping the helpee going. The helper can say, for example, "And?" "Then, what?" "But?"

The effect of focusing on helpees is that the method tends to reduce confusion, diffusion, and vagueness. Again, the ultimate outcome expected is more meaningful verbalization, and eventually, increased understanding. Another immediate outcome expected from leads focusing on feelings is that the helpee will talk more about his feeling experiences. This skill, like all in the leading cluster, has a controlling effect on the helpee. This awareness should result in cautious judgment about the degree of leading the helper should exert.

In summary, guidelines for focusing are:

1. Use your *own feelings* of confusion and sense of helpee direction as a guide to decide when to focus.
2. Be alert to *feedback* from the helpee about priority of topics.
3. Assist the helpee to *focus on feelings* which may be hidden in the discussion.

QUESTIONING

Many of the leads described above have been illustrated in the form of open questions which lead the helpee to further exploration. Such questions are not those used to obtain information nor those which can be answered with "yes" or "no." They are open-ended questions that leave the helpee free to explore and to take the interview where he wishes, rather than into areas of helper interest. This method of questioning assumes that the questions are to assist the helpee to understand rather than to promote the helper's understanding.

An example of an open question is "Could you explain more about your relationships with your parents?" *not,* "Do you get along well with your parents?" Other examples are: "What do you mean by 'failure'?" "How do they indicate their feelings?" Note that questions beginning with "how" or "what" tend to elicit elaborated responses. The effect is different from those starting with "are," "is," or "do." It would be difficult to answer the illustrative questions above with a single helpee "yes" or "no."

The following list summarizes guidelines for question types of leads:

1. Ask *open-ended questions* which cannot be answered with "yes" or "no."
2. Ask questions that elicit *feelings* from what the helpee just said rather than information.
3. Ask questions that lead to *clarification for the helpee* rather than information for the helper.

Skill cluster 3: Reflecting

Reflecting is one way of expressing to the helpee that we are in his internal frame of reference and that we recognize his deep concerns. There are three areas of reflecting—feeling, experience, and content. The main purpose of using reflection from the helper's viewpoint is to understand the helpee's experience, and to tell him that he is trying to perceive the world the way the helpee is viewing it.

REFLECTING FEELINGS

Reflecting feelings involves expressing in fresh words the essential feelings, stated or strongly implied, of the helpee. The purpose of reflecting feelings are to focus on feeling rather than content, to bring vaguely expressed feelings into clearer awareness, and to assist the helpee to "own" his feelings. So often helpees talk about their feelings as "it" or "them," as if feelings were not part of themselves. This is why we usually begin the reflecting method with *"You* feel . . ." as an attempt to help him reown the feeling. You will know when your reflection is accurate because the helpee will tend to respond with something like, "Yeah, that's it."

Skillful use of reflecting depends on the helper's ability to identify feelings and cues for feelings. He must experience feelings himself and be in touch with those feelings. Feelings are more subtle than emotions, which we usually think of as anger, love, disgust, fear, or aggression.

Examples of feelings would be affection, pleasure, hostility, guilt or anxiety. When a helpee is expressing strong emotion it is so obvious to both that reflecting is unnecessary. The more subtle feelings however, are often disguised behind words. The helper looks for these hidden feelings and brings them out in the open for the helpee to recognize more clearly.

Examples of reflecting feelings are: "In other words, you hate his guts." "You've always wanted to be a doctor." "He makes you feel guilty all the time." "It really hurts to be rejected by someone you love." Sometimes two contradictory (ambivalent) feelings are expressed, and a reflection clarifies this condition as, "He makes you angry when he punishes you, yet you feel relieved about it, too."

REFLECTING EXPERIENCE

Reflecting experience goes beyond reflecting verbalized feelings in that the helper reads the body language that is expressing implied feeling nonverbally. He responds to the *total* experience he observes in the helpee. The helper notes, for example, the rapidity of speech, the heavy breathing, sighing, flushing, changing postures, and darting glances as cues to the helpee's feeling. When reflecting feelings implied in body language, it is a good idea to describe some observed behavior first, then reflect the feeling. Examples are, "You are smiling (behavior description); but I sense you are really hurting inside" (reflection of feeling). "You say you really care about her (description); but almost every time you talk about her you clench your fists (description); it seems you strongly resent her" (feeling).

REFLECTING CONTENT

Reflecting content is repeating in fewer and fresher words the essential ideas of the helpee, and is like paraphrasing. It is used to clarify ideas that the helpee is expressing with difficulty and resulting confusion. He may lack vocabulary, for example, to express ideas simply and clearly; so, reflecting content is a skill to give him words for expressing himself. Sometimes it helps to repeat the helpee's statement, emphasizing a key word. The helpee says, for example, "Her remark really cut me." The helper responds, "It *really* hurt."

The three reflecting skills are presented together because in actual practice they blend into one another. The helper is paying attention to *what* the helpee is saying (content), but also *how* he is saying it (feeling tone). The helper usually responds with a mix of feeling and content to suit his process goals at that moment. He may judge, for example, that the helpee is not ready to face his deeper feelings implied in his body language, so he will emphasize more of the content in his reflections. It is a way of controlling feeling awareness and expression in the helping interview. On the other hand, in the early stages he may wish to emphasize recognition and exploration of feelings, so he will emphasize reflection of the total feeling impressions he gets from feeling words and observations of body movements and postures.

The helpee experiences the reflecting helper as a person who understands what he, the helpee, is experiencing. This adds considerably to the possibility that the long range outcomes of understanding self and others will be reached. A more immediate outcome is that the helpee will be able to identify and express feelings more effectively. Furthermore, he will be able to own his feelings as indicated by more "I feel" statements. In other words, he will be more ready to continue expressing feelings.

COMMON ERRORS IN REFLECTING

Some common errors in using reflecting methods are, first, getting into a rut, or *stereotyping* your responses. This means that helpers tend to begin their reflections in the same monotonous way, such as, "You feel . . .", "You think . . .", "It seems to you . . .", "I gather that . . .". This style rut tends to give the impression of insincerity or an impoverished word supply The implication is clear that we need to vary our styles of reflecting.

Another error is *timing*. Beginning helpers sometimes get into a pattern of reflecting after almost every statement the helpee makes, or they wait for a long monologue to finish and then try heroically to capture the complex feelings in one statement. It is not necessary to reflect every statement, yet it is effective to interrupt the helpee occasionally to reflect. Usually it helps to nod acceptance or give a slight "uh huh" or "I see," to encourage continuation until a reflection seems appropriate.

Overshooting with too much *depth* of feeling for which the helpee is unprepared may retard the interview. We may read more interpretations into his statements than are there. The helpee says, for example, "I don't know if I can stay overseas for a year without her." The helper who read more depth of feeling than was there responded, "You feel you can't function at all unless she is with you."

The *language* must be appropriate to the cultural experience and educational level of the helpee. He says, "I can't make it with girls; I'm so shy." The helper rather *in*appropriately responds, "Your inferiority complex really shows with girls then." At the same time the language of reflection must be natural for the helper too. If he is a traditional type, for example, he would appear as a phoney to use "mod" language.

It may be reassuring to realize that helpees usually are not as critical as these illustrations imply. As helpers, we can be wide of the mark in reflecting, but if our sincerity and interest shines through, helpees are amazingly tolerant of bungling efforts. Occasionally, an inaccurate reflection will elicit a correcting response from the helpee so that the net effect is clarification and progress even though the reflection was not accurate.

A summary of guidelines for reflecting is as follows:

1. Read the *total message*—stated feelings, nonverbal body feelings, and content.
2. Select the best *mix* of content and feelings to fulfill the goals for understanding at this stage of the helping process.
3. *Reflect* the experience just perceived.
4. *Wait* for helpee's confirming or disconfirming response to your reflection as a cue about what to do next.

Skill cluster 4: Summarizing   *Chear says we talked abt abt of topics*

Summarizing skills include attention to *what* the helpee says (content), *how* he says it (feelings), and the *purpose, timing,* and *effect* of his statements (process). It is commonplace in most helping interviews to wander widely over many ideas and feelings. This may be part of the helpee's manner of showing his discomfort by resisting direct discussion, or of keeping the helper at a safe emotional distance for awhile. It may reflect also the helpee's unwillingness to terminate the interview. Summarizing still involves a process of tying together into one statement several ideas and feelings at the end of a discussion unit or the end of an interview. It is much broader, therefore, than paraphrasing a basic message as indicated in the following example. Following a discussion of the helpee's vague feelings of inadequacy the helper says, "From your talk about family, school, and now your new job of selling, you appear to have experienced feelings of personal failure in all of them."

Summaries of an interview, or series of contacts, may include a paragraph, but the idea is to pick out the highlights and general themes of the content and feelings. Summaries of *process* include statements of where the helping process has been going and where it is now. The helper may say, for example, "You've been discussing your ideal jobs and what things you have liked and disliked about your past work; you've also talked about your plans for more training. Are you ready to take a look at some other considerations in planning for a new career?"

The main *purpose* of summarizing is to give the helpee a feeling of movement in exploring ideas and feelings, as well as awareness of progress in learning and problem solving. Summarizing also helps to finish an interview on a natural note, to clarify and focus a series of scattered ideas, and to clear the way to go on to a new idea. It permits the helpee to put the pieces together. Summarizing has the effect also of reassuring the helpee that you have been tuned in to his messages all along. For the helper it serves as an effective check on his accuracy of perceiving the full spectrum of helpee messages. Summarizing the previous sessions at the beginning of an interview often provides needed continuity.

The helper tries to get the helpee to do the summarizing, if possible. This is a test of his understanding as well as a method of keeping responsibility on him. The helper may say, for example, "How does our work look to you at this point? Try to pull it together briefly." "Let's take a look at what we've accomplished in this interview; how does it appear to you?" In terminating a relationship it is likely that the summarizing will be a joint effort to capture the essential points explored, progress achieved, and next steps planned.

Guidelines for summarizing are:

1. *Attend* to the various *themes* and emotional *overtones* as the helpee speaks.
2. Put together the key ideas and feelings into *broad statements* of his basic meanings.
3. *Do not add* new ideas to the summary.
4. *Decide* if it would be more helpful to state your summary or ask him to summarize the basic themes, agreements, or plans.
5. In deciding how to do four above consider your *purpose:*
    Was it to *warm up* the helpee at the beginning of the interview?
    Was it to *focus* his scattered thoughts and feelings?
    Was it to *close* discussion on this theme?
    Was it to *check* your understanding of the interview progress?
    Was it to *encourage* him to explore the theme more completely?
    Was it to *terminate* the relationship with a progress summary?
    Was it to *assure* him that the interview was moving along well?

Skill cluster 5: Confronting

Confronting is a complex cluster of helping skills consisting of:

1. *Recognizing* feelings in oneself as a helper.
2. *Describing* feelings in oneself and sharing them with the helpee.

3. *Feeding back* reactions in the form of *opinions* about his behavior.
4. *Meditating* as a form of self-confrontation.
5. *Repeating* as a form of emphasizing and clarifying.
6. *Associating* as a method of getting in touch with feelings.

The idea of confronting is to honestly and directly recognize and point out to helpees what is going on or what you infer is going on. The effects are challenge, exposure, or threat. Resulting emotional effects are sometimes anxiety when challenged with feedback from the helper, and sometimes pleasure with his honest opinions and expressions of caring. In other word, confronting skills involve risk—resulting either in unwanted resistance from helpees or in desired openness of communication. It is a kind of "telling it like it is" method which may threaten or thrill, depending on the timing and readiness of the helpee to be confronted with feedback honestly offered. We will look at the subskills of the confronting skill cluster in more detail below.

RECOGNIZING FEELING

It is very apparent in helping relationships that one's ability to recognize and respond to feelings in helpees is based upon the ability to recognize feelings in oneself. The helper must hear what awareness of his own inner experience is telling him. What do his tenseness, sweating palms, twitching muscles, and fluttering eyelids tell him about his own anxiety, guilt, anger, pleasure, or pain? Therefore, the helper must be aware of fine shades of feeling in himself. These feelings frequently are reactions to what the helpee is saying and can serve as guides to responses. If the helper experiences annoyance, for example, at what the helpee is saying, he must decide whether the goals of the relationship would be enhanced or retarded by expressing those feelings. As indicated in earlier discussions of countertransference feelings, the helper must make two judgments: Is this feeling of annoyance indicative of problems I have as a person, or is it a reasonable reaction to what the helpee is saying? Depending on his theory of what is helpful, the helper usually *expresses* the feeling he is aware of experiencing since the helpee senses it anyway from cues like frowns and agitation.

DESCRIBING AND SHARING FEELING

The principal value in describing feelings in oneself as a helper is that such a description helps to clarify how the helper feels. It also serves as a *model* for the helpee to recognize and express his feelings. Helpees frequently do not understand the idea of expressing feeling, especially to near strangers—as helpers often appear initially to them. The condition of *trust* is dependent on an open sharing of feelings. Again, the helper can accelerate the process of building trust by sharing his own feelings. This "sharing of experience" as described in Brammer and Shostrom (1968) is one of the best ways to model the idea of "being a person." Some examples are the helper saying, "Your continuing on and on like that is boring me and I find myself getting sleepy." "I feel angry when you talk so much about wanting to hurt other people and not giving a damn about them." "It makes me feel good when you talk about yourself that way." You can see that this kind of response could have a reinforcing effect on the helpee, because he is getting some rewards in the form of helper response for expressing feelings even when that response has a critical tone.

The *values for the helpee* of sharing feelings are considerable. He experiences relief from the tension, (sometimes called emotional catharsis), satisfaction that he had the courage to face the feeling, and release of new creative energy.

The *limitations* of free expression of feelings by helpees (often called ventilation) are that he feels so good afterward that he considers it is unnecessary to go on actively solving his problems. Sometimes, as we will see in the next chapter, expression of feeling is a goal in itself to provide relief from suffering. Most helpees have protective mechanisms for preventing them from revealing more feeling than they are able to tolerate, and helpers should be alert to occasions when it is not so. There are times when the helpee's defenses are overwhelmed, so to speak, and where his behavior deteriorates under prolonged emotional catharsis. This is why it is necessary for helpers offering their services to have colleagues, or specialist referral resources, to call upon in such emergencies.

Some guidelines for knowing how far to let helpees ventilate and some cautions to observe follow. Be cautious about free expression of feeling if:

1. he is known to have severe emotional disorders—hysterical tendencies, delusional thinking, extreme anger, for example;
2. his life is frought with crises and emotionally demanding pressures such that discussing them mobilizes more feeling than he can handle;
3. his past history in dealing with emotional crises is known to be shaky;
4. strong resistance to exploration of feelings is noted;
5. adequacy of your own experience as a helper of disturbed people is doubtful;
6. your own emotional life is in turmoil;

7. time available for working through the feelings all the way is not adequate;
8. specialist support services are not available or adequate;
9. policies of your agency for exploring intense emotional life of clients is discouraged;
10. attitudes and expectations of parents or guardians of young helpees are not explored.

These guidelines are included to enhance your awareness of possible hazards in free expression of feeling, not to discourage you nor make you fearful about dealing with helpee feelings, and also because of the common idea in helping circles that sharing strong feelings always has desirable outcomes. If you find that sharing your own feelings, or working with helpees who are sharing their feelings, is uncomfortable or interferes with your effectiveness, it is a signal to do more work on your own feelings through means described in chapter 2.

An issue more common than excessive sharing of feelings is the helpee's underexpression or ignoring of his feelings. This condition is manifested when the helper focuses on *content* or when the helpee uses the phrase "I feel . . ." when he is referring to an idea. Thus, he is unaware that he is avoiding feelings. An example is, "I feel that the best thing to do is not to go to college at this time." Depending on the tone, this statement expresses an opinion or a conclusion rather than a feeling. A feeling statement would be more like, "I'm afraid of going to college now. High school was such a bore." The principal goal of the helper in using the confronting skill is to challenge the helpee to include honest feeling in his statements. One of the keys to this condition is to model expression of feeling yourself.

A confrontive way to get helpees to express feelings is to ask them to do so. Some examples are: "What are you feeling right now?" "You've described some facts about your situation; how do you feel about it?" "You have been saying how you feel about your job, but I haven't sensed your true feelings about it yet. How strongly do you feel about it?"

In summary, guidelines for describing and sharing feelings are:

1. *Share* your own feelings as a model.
2. *Ask* the helpee to share his feelings.
3. Be *cautious* about the depth and extent of sharing.

FEEDBACK AND OPINION

One of the most confrontive skills is honest reaction to the helpee on how he affects you. Its value lies in its potential for enabling the helpee to understand himself and to change his behavior. We acquire our definitions of who we are by the reactions of other people to us. Our personalities are the total of our parents' opinions, chidings, and praises. Our helping relationships merely continue this basic process in a more focused fashion.

Feedback is a term borrowed from electronics and physics where information is fed back into a system so that corrections can be made. Examples are thermostats which use information about temperature to activate the furnace switch, or guidance systems in space vehicles which feed information into the navigation equipment to correct the astronauts' course. Similarly, we give information in the form of opinions and reactions to helpees. As a result, they have a better idea of how they are performing, and they can use the information, if they so wish, to change their behavior. Reactions from others are the means for establishing our identity and answering the question, "Who am I?" The main *guidelines* for giving feedback are:

1. Give opinions in the form of feedback only when the helpee is *ready*. This means that in most cases he will ask for feedback, but if not, the helper will ask if he would like some of his reactions. An example is, "We have been talking about your plans for the future, while you were listing your limitations I had some reactions." (Helpee's interest is aroused and he responds, "Oh . . . tell me.") "Well, I'm convinced from what you have told me about yourself that you are vastly underestimating your capabilities here; from my observations I think you express yourself very clearly and concisely, for example."

Feedback may be in the form of critical commentary, also, as in the following illustration: "We have been talking about your problems in getting along with people. You may be interested to know that I have been feeling increasingly irritated with your persistent quibbling about almost everything I say. I feel that I don't want to listen to you anymore. Do you think my reaction is typical of those of other people you know?"

Giving opinions without helpee readiness to make use of them is only likely to arouse resistance, resentment toward the helper, or outright denial since it would not fit the helpee's current opinion of himself.

2. *Describe the behavior* before giving your reaction to it. Note in the illustrations above that the helper described the specific instance and then gave his feeling about it. This keeps the responsibility for opinions on yourself. Often it is difficult to determine when the feedback is a projection of your personal prejudices and problems and when it is the kind of reaction that the helpee generally would get from people. This is why the feedback type of confronting must be done with caution, tentativeness, and the clear understanding that the helper is offering his *personal*

reactions to the helpee's behavior. Keeping your reactions descriptive rather than evaluative leaves the helper free to use them as he sees fit.

3. Give feedback in the form of *opinions about his behavior* rather than judgments about him. It may seem like quibbling to separate his behavior from him as a person, but it is vastly different to say, "I don't like the way you constantly interrupt me," from "I don't like you because you are constantly interrupting me."

4. Give feedback about things that the helpee has the *capacity to change*. It is not helpful to give feedback about physical characteristics or life circumstances, for example, which he would find very difficult to change.

5. Feedback should be *given in small amounts* so that the helpee can experience the full impact of the helper's reaction. Too many items may overload him and create confusion and possible resentment. An example of such an overload would be, "I didn't like the way you spoke to me; I felt put down. Besides, you have been late consistently to our staff meetings and your progress reports have been getting skimpier which has been irritating me even more." Feedback given in this cumulative manner serves more as ventilation of hostility for the giver, and less as a helpful gesture to the helpee.

6. Feedback should be a *prompt response* to current and specific behavior, not unfinished emotional business from the past. Being told, for example, that he is "too forceful" is not as helpful as saying, "Just as we were about to decide what to do, you pushed your idea and seemed not to hear the other suggestions. I was conflicted about whether to resist you or just give in."

7. Ask the helpee for *reactions* to your feedback. Was it helpful or not? Did it enhance the relationship or diminish it?

MEDITATING

Meditating is a form of self-confrontation which has ancient origins. Many philosophical groups in the Orient such as Zen, Yoga, and Sufi, along with the Christian and Hebrew traditions of the West, emphasize the values of self-understanding inherent in meditational forms. The main feature and principal value of meditation for the helping process is that it stops the active flow of ideas and actions. It is a kind of "stop time" where the helpee can get in touch with himself. Meditation opens the possibilities of awareness of self in relation to the world, which is different from the usual rational sensory types of awareness. Our Western languages have few forms in which to express these nonrational or esoteric experiences. Zen, for example, emphasizes awareness through a state of "no mind" where the flow of consciousness stops. Various styles of meditation are aided by special postures, mantras (repeated vocalizations), contemplating an object, or breathing exercises, but the basic idea of stopping action and thought to allow other forms of experience is the same among them.

If you decide that this meditational form of self-confrontation would be useful to your helpees, you should become familiar with at least one of the styles mentioned above and experience it first yourself. There are a few general principles which can help, even if you are relatively unsophisticated about specific meditational forms. A helpee who is flitting from topic to topic and who is having difficulty getting in touch with his feelings, for example, might be helped through some kind of meditation. You can ask your helpee to stop talking, close his eyes, get in a comfortable position, and just be quiet awhile. You might ask him to focus on his breathing—how he inhales and exhales and to let the ideas flitting across his awareness just fade away.

The value for the helpee of this method is that it should open new doors to his feelings and awareness of himself in relation to others and his physical environment. If nothing else, it should help him to calm down and should prepare him for a new approach to his problems. To obtain maximum value from meditational methods, helpees should practice them in everyday life.

Here is a summary of guidelines for using meditational forms of self-confrontation:

1. Be familiar with one or more styles through *personal experience*.
2. *Explain* the value of the method to the helpee.
3. Ask him to assume a relaxed *comfortable position* with eyes closed.
4. Ask him to be *quiet* and to let his thoughts fade away.
5. Ask him to focus on his *breathing* as a means of getting in touch with his body processes and feelings.
6. After a few minutes ask him to open his eyes and *describe the experience* using leads from feeling statements to encourage further exploration.
7. Ask him to *practice* this confrontational form at home if he finds it productive and satisfying.

REPEATING

Repeating is another method of self-confrontation, prompted by the helper, which comes out of the Gestalt tradition. He asks the helpee to merely repeat a word, phrase, or short sentence one or more times. The helper suggests that the helpee focus on one of his statements that appears to have intense meaning for him. The helper then asks him to repeat it in simple direct form. The purpose is to generate more feelings associated with those words as the repetitions continue. The helper asks him to try to hear what he is saying emotionally with the repetitions. Then either they discuss the feelings precipitated or the feeling spills out in a form such as tears.

The value for the helpee of this kind of confronting is that he can tap feelings that are obscured behind long sentences and constant topic changes. It breaks up his usual method of discourse suddenly, which usually serves to provoke intense feelings. The simplicity of the repetition method evokes little resistance from the helpee. It puts him into a simple childlike frame of thinking which cuts through his sophisticated adult verbiage. Finally, it offers to the helpee a means of focusing on significant feelings and of avoiding the temptation to move quickly on to safer topics.

The judgment involved is knowing when to ask the helpee to repeat and then simply asking him to "Say it again," assisting him with further requests simply as, "Again . . . again." This process is continued until the feeling comes out in verbal or nonverbal form such as crying or striking. The same process can be used with gestures. If you see the helpee shaking his fist, for example, you might ask him to "Do that again." It focuses his attention on the emotional impact of the gesture. An example of the repeating method of self-confrontation is:

He: I don't have any friends; people don't love me, I guess.

Hr: Say that again, "People don't love me."

He: People don't love me. People don't love me. (Pause) Maybe I'm not very lovable.

Hr: Say again, "I'm not lovable."

He: I'm not lovable.

Hr: Again.

He: I'm not lovable.

This kind of repeating opens the possibilities for significant confrontation of self-regarding attitudes that are hindering effective personal and interpersonal functioning. It brings painful feelings to the point where they can be discussed directly.

Guidelines for the repeating method are:

1. Note *statements* or *gestures* with feeling implications.
2. Ask the helpee to *repeat* the key word, phrase, or short sentence one or more times until feelings are evoked.
3. *Encourage* the helpee to keep the repetition in the present active verb tense.

4. Allow sufficient *time* for the emotional impact to be felt and sorted out meaningfully by the helpee before going on to another topic.

ASSOCIATING

Associating is another skill to facilitate the loosening of feelings. It is a more precise form of the old "free association" method where the helpee was encouraged to say whatever crossed his awareness. The goal was to get the helpee loosened from his precise, logical, planned statements and into the more fragmentary and illogical realm of feelings. You suggest, for example, "Tell me what is on your mind, and say it even if it seems vague and unimportant." "Let yourself go." "Just give me pieces of ideas; don't try to be logical."

Another variation of associating method is to pick out a word from the helpee's statements that seems to have emotional significance for him. You then ask him to let himself go with the word and give all the other words that come to awareness in rapid order. You note them for discussion later. An example is:

Hr: You seem to be fixed on your mother's influence on you. I suggest that you say the word "mother" and follow it with as many words as you can think of in rapid order. Do you understand?
He: Yes, I think so. Mother—love, soft, fun, spank . . . .

The main outcome expected for helpees is a freeing of feelings so they are more available for direct discussion. It also gets to feelings faster than usual discussion methods.

In summary, guidelines for association skills are:

1. Ask the helpee to *say what comes* to his awareness.
2. *Explain* that the flowing ideas do not need to be logical or consistent.
3. *Use the results* to aid the helpee into further exploration of feelings or discussion of the results of his associating.
4. As a variation, *pick out a word* with possible emotional significance from the helpee's statements and ask him to say freely all the thoughts and feelings evoked by that word as fast as they come.

Skill cluster 6: Interpreting

Interpreting is an active helper process of explaining the meaning of events to helpees so that they are able to see their problems in new ways. The main goal is to teach helpees to interpret events in their lives by themselves. In *paraphrasing,* the helpee's internal frame of reference is maintained, whereas, through *interpretation* the helper offers a new frame of reference. Interpretation is used more in formal psychotherapy than in simpler styles of helping because of the therapist's need to think diagnostically. He must be formulating hunches all the time about what is going on and what might be a logical explanation for this helpee's behavior. He does not always share these thoughts since they serve primarily to help him understand what is going on in the helpee. Many helpers feel this kind of thinking gets in the way of the helping process because the helper becomes preoccupied with thinking *about* or *ahead* of the helpee rather than *with* him. This shift to the external frame of reference in the helper is one of the main limitations of using interpretive skills.

Helpers need to be constantly alert to the meanings of the behavior they observe, but they must strive also to keep in touch with where the helpee is now, emotionally and intellectually. Examples are those situations when the helpee is describing his behavior such as theft, and you have a hunch as to some of the underlying factors motivating this behavior. He may be describing his anger toward his wife's dominating behavior. You have noted his earlier statements about similar feelings toward his mother. You now hypothesize a connection between the two feelings. You keep these hunches to yourself as an hypothesis, look for more supporting data, and then, when the relationship is well-established and your hunch has more support, you might offer it to the helpee as an interpretation. Until this time all diagnostic and interpretive thinking is for the helper himself.

The explanations in interpretation often are given in terms of some special theory of personality change held by the helper. Usually these explanations are expressed as hypotheses or hunches about what is happening. These are the reasons why there are so many styles of interpreting. Seeing filmed or taped examples is the best method of becoming familiar with these styles, because interpretation is no single simple skill which can be illustrated by a short excerpt.

Interpreting is closely related to reflecting, the main difference being that interpreting adds the helper's meanings to the helpee's basic message. The final decision about the usefulness of an interpretation is whether it aids the helpee to understand himself or his problems more clearly, and then whether this understanding prompts him to act more effectively.

When you decide that an interpretation might be helpful, look for the basic message of the helpee (as in reflecting and paraphrasing), restate it in capsule form, then add your understanding of what the helpee has said (the interpreting). If the interpretation makes sense to the helpee it will accelerate the interview. If the interpretation is not meaningful, try again. You must also be confident that your interpretation was essentially accurate, since it may take some time before its significance to the helpee sinks in. Interpreting means that you are out in front leading him to seek wider understandings of his feelings and broader perceptions. You must recognize that occasionally you will be way out there by yourself, and that then you will need to try again a little closer to the helpee's level of awareness. It should be understood clearly that the *goal* of all interpretive effort is *self-interpretation* by the helpee.

Some examples of interpretation at a simple level without an elaborate theoretical rationale are: "You have told me about your family as if you were a disinterested observer. You have no specific feeling about them then?" "It is possible for a person to both love and hate his father at the same time?" "I wonder if you see that your feelings of hostility toward men might be at the root of your marital difficulties?"

INTERPRETIVE QUESTIONS

Some interpreting is done in the form of questions such as, "Do you think then that you distrust women because your mother treated you so badly?" This questioning form implies a more tentative quality than the more declarative statements and makes interpreting less risky for the helper. Interpretive questions have a focusing effect also, such as in the following illustration where the helpee has been avoiding discussion of his self-concerns.

Hr: When are you going to be concerned about yourself too?
He: That is a selfish attitude.
Hr: So, what's wrong with that?
He: I don't like selfish people.
Hr: Because . . . ?
He: Selfish people aren't very popular.
Hr: So, popularity is important to you; and if you are too self-centered, people won't like you. Is that getting close to where you are?

FANTASY AND METAPHOR INTERPRETATIONS

Another stylized way of introducing an interpretation is to put it in the form of a fantasy (daydream), even using picture language like a metaphor. An example is, "I have a fantasy about what you have just said. I picture you walking down a path in the woods, coming to a fork in the path, and being undecided which one to choose. You unconcernedly flip a coin and run joyfully down the path chosen by the coin. How does this fit?" Hopefully, the fantasy is close to his awareness and triggers new ways of perceiving himself through further discussion. The limitation is that in using this skill the helper shifts all the way into his frame of reference, thus forcing the helpee to deal with him (or his fantasy). Sometimes it is useful just to give one's reaction in the form of a metaphor, such as, "Most of the time I perceive you as a great big soft teddy bear who stays in any position he is placed."

I have mentioned the idea of *levels* of interpreting several times. Interpreting could be placed on a continuum from reflecting, where you stay at the meaning and feeling level of the helpee, through elaborate theoretical explanation of his behavior in depth interpretation. Even in so-called "depth" interpretation we do not dig deeply into the helpee's psyche and come up with brilliant insights which unfold the mysteries of his personality. This is the popular view that came from distorted perceptions of psychoanalytic methods. There are levels of meaning however, in interpretive methods. The following illustration offers a few of these ways of responding at different levels. The helpee says, "I was at a party last night where I drank too much. I broke into tears and cried and cried. I acted like a child who wanted to go home to mother. I feel so ashamed." Your response, at different levels, might be one of the following:

1. You drank to the point where tears came freely. You're ashamed now as you talk about it. (content paraphrase)
2. You feel very badly about what happened last night. (general feeling reflection)
3. You feel badly that you lost control of yourself last night. (mild interpreting—adding the idea of control)
4. You drank until you lost control of your feelings. As you look back on the evening now you want to punish yourself for acting that childish way. (interpreting—adding idea of punishing and reverting to childhood patterns)
5. Your drinking, crying, and mentioning mother, makes me wonder if you want to go back to mother—like being dependent on her for comfort and feeling you can't stand on your own two feet. (deeper level interpreting—desire for a comforting mother and dependency)
6. (Interpreting his statement according to some theoretical framework, like Gestalt, which might explain in terms of giving up dependency on others and substituting self-dependency; or the Rational-Emotive approach for getting rid of self-defeating and self-punishing feelings about one's behavior; or Psychoanalytic interpretations

about wishes to go back to the womb. Behaviorally oriented helpers
might inquire about the helpee's desire to change his drinking
or crying behavior.)

There are myriads of verbal forms for couching interpreting skills.
The topic is really too complex to cover in detail in this basic helping
skills book, but it would be wrong to understate the significance and
usefulness of interpreting skill for the average helper. We should know
not only the possible uses, but also the implications for misuse. Further
readings in the references at the end of this chapter will add to your
understanding of various styles of interpretation.

The main consequences for the helpee of being confronted through
interpretation are broadened perceptions of meaning of his behavior and
different ways of viewing his problem and possible solutions. Generally
speaking, the helpee can expect a deeper understanding of his problem
as a result of the added perspectives of the helper. If you get the "Suddenly, I realized . . ." reaction, you know your interpreting has been
successful. Interpreting also has the effect of intensifying the emotional
involvement of the helpee so that he will take more responsibility for his
own interpreting.

Guidelines for interpreting are:

1. Look for the *basic message(s)* of the helpee.
2. *Paraphrase* these to him.
3. Add *your understanding* of what his message means in terms of
   your theory or your general explanation of motives, defenses, needs,
   styles, etc.
4. Keep the *language simple* and the *level close to his message.* Avoid
   wild speculation and statements in esoteric words.
5. *Introduce* your ideas with some kind of statement indicating that
   you are offering *your ideas tentatively* on what his words or behavior
   means. Examples are: "Is this a fair statement . . . ?" "The way
   I see it is . . ." "I wonder if . . . " "Try this one on for size . . ."
6. Solicit the *helpee's reactions* to your interpretations.
7. Your main goal is to *teach the helpee* to do his own interpreting.
   Remember, you can't give insight to others.

Skill cluster 7: Informing

This skill of information-giving is so commonplace that it needs no
elaboration. It is included here to indicate that there are times when
sharing simple facts possessed by the helper is the most helpful thing he
could do. There are some kinds of information in the expertise category,

such as information from test instruments. The special skills required in this type of helping for planning and decision making are beyond the scope of this general helping book. Further information may be obtained about skills for informing about interests, aptitudes, and personality traits from Brammer and Shostrom (1968) and the suggested readings section at the end of this chapter.

There is another category of information about services to solve the myriads of human problems from financial planning, to career planning, to family planning which need to be handled by specially informed people through referral skills to be described in the next chapter.

ADVICE

There is a common type of informing activity by helpers called *advice giving*. The helper is thrust into the role of the expert in so many areas by helpees who expect some kind of expert pronouncements in the form of sound advice on what to do. A common experience of beginning helpers is to perceive their function as giving "common sense" advice.

There is a long tradition of advice giving in the helping folklore. It is a common occurrence between persons who know and trust one another. This time-honored function among friends is often beneficial. Issues arise, however, when a helpee consults a helper in his larger environment at work, church, or school. These institutions have many natural self-styled advice givers who often have attractive charismatic qualities. As a consequence, they are sought out by confused and troubled people, largely because they are attractive people with a reputation for being helpful. These persons could just as well be janitors or clerks as well as those with titles such as minister or teacher. Helpees without serious emotional disabilities often do not want psychotherapy or counseling, but seek advice mainly on a particular problem. What they often search for is an empathic listener who will not attempt to "psych them out," "play the therapy game," or become a psychological version of "wet nurse."

In an informal study of what Korner * called "indigenous counselors" he found that almost all bureaucratic organizations had such an informally appointed advice-giver in the small group structures. This person's function, according to Korner's data, is to become the organization's human behavior lay-expert. His data from people who consulted these indigenous advisers indicate that such advisers enjoy talking to people, appreciate the respect and confidence people place in them, appear self-

* Korner, I. Unpublished paper "About Advice Giving."

confident and dignified, are very willing to give of their store of accumulated problem-solving experience in a no-nonsense neutral manner. They had an unusual quality to get to the core of the matter and inspire confidence and trust. The advice was offered in a manner which did not obligate the receiver to follow it or seek subsequent meetings for further help. Receivers were careful to indicate that this adviser was not the same kind of person who offered solace and support to reduce psychic discomfort. The main contributions of the indigenous advice-givers were to crystallize and focus issues, to clarify decision processes, and to move beyond the impasse. It appears that persons perceived as helpful "advice-givers" use helping skills far beyond sheer conventional advice. These findings suggest also that such indigenous helpers in organizations are performing useful services to people informally and could probably enhance their effectiveness with additional work on helping skills. Unfortunately, Korner's data did not reveal the nature or the consequences of "bad advice."

Giving advice in the traditional manner is a controversial topic in helping literature. Some writers condemn advice dispensing as a counseling tool without reservation. Critics claim advising reflects some arrogance of the helper who assumes he is so all-knowing that he can advise another person on a course of action. Critics also claim ineffectiveness and fostering of dependency. Others assert that advice-giving is helpful under some circumstances. Advice can be helpful if it is given by trusted persons with expert opinions based on solid knowledge of a supporting field such as law, medicine, or childrearing. Sometimes helpees need a recommended course of action supported by wide experience, and hopefully, facts. There is a place for suggestions which leave their evaluation and the final decision about courses of action completely open to the helpee. You can suggest "hunches" or "hypotheses" that need checking before acting. You can suggest ways of approaching problems. Examples are situations in which parents are exploring ways of handling rebellious children or students are weighing choices about courses. The use of considered suggestions is appropriate when the contact is short and the decision relatively inconsequential in the person's life.

Advice is often appropriate in crisis situations where several people must cooperate to prepare helpees for major readjustments of their life circumstances, such as family reorganization after hospitalization, divorce, imprisonment, unemployment, or financial loss. Advice is wholly inappropriate for dealing with major individual choice questions, such as, "Should I get a divorce," or "What career should I enter?"

Most people object to advice given in the form of "father knows best," or offhand suggestions tempered with strong persuasion. Usually, the person giving the advice has a strong stake in the helpee's following his advice so he puts some persuasive punch into it. This attitude often generates hostility in helpees.

The principal limitation of advice giving is that helpees usually don't follow it. They often seemingly ask, or even beg, for advice but they are most often asking themselves the rhetorical question, "What shall I do?" They may be expressing dependent feelings, knowing full well what to do, actionwise. If the helper falls into this trap he justifiably incurs the wrath or contempt of the helpee. A more productive strategy, especially if there is time, is to deal with the feelings involved first. The main task is to distinguish between the honest and direct request for information or suggestions and the expression of indecisive or dependent feelings. When in doubt, it is more productive to try a reflecting approach with the presumed feelings first, and then deal with the request itself.

Some other limitations of giving advice are that they reinforce dependency on experts which shifts responsibility to the helper for solutions. Frequently, the helper who takes the "If I were you . . ." approach is projecting his own needs, problems, or values into the advice rather than keeping the helpee's needs foremost. Experience in group forms of helping indicates that when participants begin giving advice they often do so because they unconsciously perceive the other person's problems as their own. Therefore, they are really speaking to themselves. Another limitation, furthermore, is that the helpee may take the helper's advice and later find that it was invalid. The helper then is blamed when things don't turn out right in the helpee's life.

A summary of guidelines for informing skills is as follows:

1. Be *informed,* or know the sources of information, in your area of advertised expertise.
2. Do not use educational or psychological test instruments without thorough *training* in their uses and limitations.
3. Don't use advice unless it is in the form of *tentative suggestions* based upon solid expertise.

Outcomes you should expect from studying this chapter

Now that you have read this chapter you should reasonably expect to: (1) list the seven main clusters of skills for promoting awareness of understanding self and environment; (2) cite subskills in the clusters and illustrate their uses and misuses with examples from helping interviews; (3) apply the skills after practice and feedback from associates according to strategies suggested in chapter 5.

Suggestions for further study

AMOS, W., and GRAMBS, J. *Counseling the Disadvantaged Youth.* Englewood Cliffs, N.J.: Prentice-Hall, 1968. (Special skills needed to work with helpees from disadvantaged groups.)

BENJAMIN, A. *The Helping Interview.* Boston: Houghton Mifflin, 1969. (Ch. 5 on the use of questions, and Ch. 7 on leading and reflecting.)

BRAMMER, L., and SHOSTROM, E. *Therapeutic Psychology: Fundamentals of Actualization Counseling and Psychotherapy.* 2nd ed. Englewood Cliffs, N. J.: Prentice-Hall, 1968. (Ch. 7 on relationship techniques, Ch. 9 on interpretation techniques, Ch. 10 on advice, information, and tests.)

GORDON, T. *Parent Effectiveness Training.* New York: Peter H. Wyden, 1970. (Chs. 3–7 on listening methods with children.)

LEVY, L. *Psychological Interpretation.* New York: Holt, Rinehart & Winston, 1963. (A detailed presentation of interpretive techniques.)

LIGON, M., and MCDANIEL, S. *The Teacher's Role in Counseling.* Englewood Cliffs, N. J.: Prentice-Hall, 1970. (Ch. 5 on the gathering and use of information.)

PEREZ, J. *The Initial Counseling Contact.* Boston: Houghton Mifflin, 1968. (Ch. 4 Practical techniques in the initial contact, Appendix A, sample of a verbatim first interview.)

ROGERS, C. *Client-Centered Therapy.* Boston: Houghton Mifflin, 1951. (Description, rationale, and illustrations of reflecting skills.)

SUPER, D., and CRITES, J. *Appraising Vocational Fitness by Means of Psychological Testing.* New York: Harper & Row, 1962. (An overview and depth study of the tests used in vocational counseling.)

7 | *Helping skills for comfort and crisis utilization*

One of the most common helping functions is providing relief from psychological suffering. Although there is a huge reservoir of human experience to draw upon, there is little aid in the way of behavioral science theory, research, and practice to understand and deal with human stress and crises. The social work literature contains many practical ideas for dealing with specific types of human crises, and traditional religions have had much to say about human suffering and crises. Darbonne (1967) has surveyed the scattered crisis literature spanning the last 20 years. He reported increasing interest among the helping professions in the area of "crisis intervention."

Although there are some special skills available for providing comfort and managing crises, the personhood, or the "self as instrument," of the helper is a more important consideration. His values, life style, and personality traits have a profound impact on the helpee's ability to face stress and crises. Thus, the helper cannot depend on his bank of skills and strategies only. Behavioral scientists who produce most of the concepts and test the methods for helper effectiveness cannot offer belief systems, values to live by, or hope to suffering persons as scientists. The helper must draw upon a variety of sources for his values, ideas, and skills. Some of these resources fall in religion, philosophy, behavioral science, and the helping professions. Many of the skills described in the previous chapter apply here, too, in that they provide support functions in addition to promoting understanding.

This chapter will (1) describe some of the outcomes you may expect from reading this chapter; (2) define and discuss some of the terms used in crisis work; (3) describe some strategies for helping people in crisis; (4) describe some skills to facilitate support in times of stress and crisis; and (5) list some suggestions for further reading.

Outcomes you can expect

From studying this chapter you will be competent to (1) identify skills and strategies useful in situations requiring support and comfort; (2) identify understanding skills that also have a supportive function; (3) use the terminology for describing crisis and stress; (4) exercise judgment on strategies to be used in stress and crisis situations. The ultimate standards of your effectiveness will be the success of your interventions, as measured by the helpee's improved ability to cope with crises, and evidence that he has learned how to utilize crises for growth in the future.

Human conditions of concern

It is difficult to classify human problems meaningfully and to separate cause and effect. Some illustrative stress and crisis conditions can be divided into three categories: loss due to outside factors, internal distress regardless of cause, and transitional states that demand adaptive responses. Some of these conditions are:

Loss

Bereavement	Divorce
Unemployment	Imprisonment
Disaster	

Internal distress

Hopelessness	Battle fatigue
Despair	Bad drug trips
Depression	Suicide attempts

Transitional states

Job change	Family conflict
Relocation	Impending threat
New family member	Illness

Hill (1958) classified stressors in family crises into external and internal factors. A stress-producing crisis that originates *outside* the family, such as war, persecution, or natural disaster often solidifies family efforts to resolve the stress. *Internal* family events, however, such as suicide, nonsupport, infidelity, or alcoholism often result in some kind of disintegrating family crisis because these behaviors reflect on the competence of the family to cope with its own affairs. Hill further classifies crises on the basis of effect on the family. Examples are (1) dismemberment (loss of family member); (2) accession (surprise addition of member); and (3) demoralization (decreased morale). Sooner or later these conditions result in a major family crisis, preceded usually by progressive disintegration. Figure 7 illustrates the wide range of problems that can precipitate family crises.

FIGURE 7.   A classification of family crises of dismemberment—accession and demoralization. (Reproduced from Hill, 1958, p. 38.)

Dismemberment only
Death of child, spouse, or parent
Hospitalization of spouse
War separation

Accession only
Unwanted pregnancy
Deserter returns
Stepfather, stepmother additions
Some war reunions
Some adoptions, aged grandparents, orphaned kin

Demoralization only
Nonsupport
Infidelity
Alcoholism
Drug addiction
Delinquency and events bringing disgrace

Demoralization plus dismemberment or accession
Illegitimacy
Runaways
Desertion
Divorce
Imprisonment
Suicide or homicide
Institutionalization for mental illness

Definition of terms

Stress. A condition characterized by physiological tension and persistent choice conflict. The helpee feels under pressure to reduce the tension and achieve comfort or equilibrium. Often the resolution takes a maladaptive form, such as illness, without awareness in the helpee. Stress is a more pervasive and less intense condition than crisis; but it may continue for unlimited time, with or without the provoking stimulus.

Crisis. A state of disorganization in which the helpee faces frustration of important life goals or profound disruption of his life cycle and methods of coping with stress. The term crisis refers usually to the helpee's feelings about the disruption, not the disruption itself. Crises are limited in time, usually lasting not more than a few weeks.

There are normal *developmental* crises, such as birth or a child going off to school. *Situational* crises are associated with severe loss of status, possessions, or loved ones. *Existential* crises refer to the conflicts and anxious feelings experienced when facing the significant human issues of purpose, responsibility, freedom, and commitment. Although this type of crisis is a normal part of human existence it becomes a true crisis when one becomes aware of old forms of constricted being and new possibilities for action. For some, these pressures to choose and to act assume crisis proportions. If they are not resolved in a constructive way through normal living or special helping processes, the crisis eventuates in feelings that range from detached boredom and purposelessness, despair over forced responsibility for choice, and finally to panic and disintegration.

Four *phases* of a crisis period have been described by Caplan (1964). An adaptation of his phases follows: (1) Initial tension is experienced, which arouses habitual adaptive responses. (2) Tension increases under continuous stimulation, and lack of success is experienced in coping and tension reduction. This frustration is complicated by distress and inefficiency. (3) Tension increases until emergency resources, internal and external, are mobilized. The crisis may be eased temporarily through such emergency coping mechanisms, seeing the problem differently, or relinquishing goals. (4) An acute phase follows if the crisis is not eased in stage 3, or averted by denial or resignation. Tension mounts to the point where major dysfunctions in behavior develop, and/or emotional control is lost.

Although a crisis state may precipitate either complete dysfunction or no observable response, it may also create the seeds of considerable growth. The helpee can be highly influenced at this stage. The *values* of crisis can be realized if the person is now ready to reach for higher levels of self-realization, as well as calm equilibrium. This is why availability of the helping process is so crucial at this early stage because the helpee is so malleable and ready for change. Parad (1965) cites many instances where agencies practicing crisis intervention have productive outcomes when the help is offered and accepted early.

In addition to the availability of helping relationships, the psychological background and makeup of the person determine to a great extent his reaction to prolonged stress and intensive crises. This is why we cannot assume when disaster strikes or a family seems to be going through enormous stress that some kind of massive help is necessary. Some persons and families have enormous reserves to draw upon.

Bloom (1963) studied the problem of how helping professionals viewed crises through scrutiny of short case histories. These histories contained varying amounts of five elements usually constituting a crisis condition: (1) awareness of the precipitating event; (2) rapidity of onset; (3) presence of discomfort; (4) external evidence of behavior disruption; and (5) rapidity of resolution. Bloom found that helpers defined a crisis largely in terms of precipitating events and to some extent on time of resolution, but a problem arose when trying to differentiate between those profound events that led to a crisis state and those that did not. This lack of precision in defining a crisis makes it very difficult to determine the effectiveness of a particular strategy or method.

Support. Support is a condition in which the helpee feels secure and comfortable psychologically. It includes awareness of well-being and satisfaction of "affect hunger." Support comes from three sources: (1) the relationship itself where the helpee experiences the helper's acceptance and warmth; (2) experiencing direct help in the form of stress reducing reassurance or environmental support; (3) experiencing the helper's assumption of major responsibility in the relationship as a temporary expedient to reduce stress. As you might have noticed from reading the above conditions of support, to encourage support actively is controversial among helpers. Some helpers claim that providing support is a necessary helping function, especially for persons in states of crisis. The helpee needs comfort and security to recoup his coping forces, and the interview definitely should not add to his stress. Others assert that deliberately providing support reduces an opportunity for growth. They claim that helpees should take advantage of the "shaken up" condition to explore new avenues of growth, take new risks, complete their "grief work" and make new plans, if the crisis involves bereavement. The psychological "first aid" should be the supportive quality of the helper's attentive and caring presence only.

One *value* of providing direct support is reduction of debilitating anxiety, and consequent psychological comfort. Helpees who feel inadequate, unworthy, grief stricken, lonely, or fearful are given a supportive helper on whom they can lean during the peak of their crisis, or the depth of their feelings, until they can marshal their strength to go on. In such a supportive relationship the helpee can feel that he does not need to be strong and capable for awhile. It is like feeling that he can "walk" before he needs to "run." Support conditions allow him to get his dependency and security needs expressed and faced.

The grief stricken person in a supportive relationship also feels that he is not alone, that someone understands, and that he is free to share his hurt. Similarly, a supportive relationship helps the person who is fearful of his impulses to feel that it is all right to express strong feelings of despair and frustration without being hurt more. Proper support also assures the helpee that he can help himself, that he is capable, that he is worthy, or that he can plan. Feeling, for example, than he can save his marriage gives him the courage to keep trying for solutions.

Finally, a supportive relationship assures the helpee that he does not need to take impulsive action which might increase his difficulties. He can take sufficient time to get his feelings sorted out and to explore alternatives before acting. An example is introducing "stop time" before initiating a divorce proceeding.

Some of the *limitations* of supportive relationships were implied above. Briefly, a major limitation is the creation of dependence on the helper as a source of support. Sometimes helpees feel resentful, or even guilty, when they are recipients of support. Occasionally they experience dependence on the helper. Some are threatened by too much warmth and closeness because they have not yet learned how to manage a close human relationship when they are hurting.

Supportive efforts come across occasionally as sympathy, which implies feeling sorry for the helpee. Efforts at sympathy are interpreted by him as insincere and gimmicky. Overuse of reassurance, for example, makes the helper especially vulnerable to reactions of shallowness from helpees. They have heard the platitude so many times that "everything will come out in the wash, so don't fret"; or "every cloud has a silver lining." He knows from experience that it is not true that things always turn out "right" or for the "best." This awareness is apparent especially when you or someone else has given the helpee some bad news. If he has received negative evaluations of his work performance, for example, he usually knows he has been unsatisfactory. There is nothing to be gained from "sweetening" the news, of assuring him that some "miracle" is going to happen, or that people do not "understand" him. A strategy likely to produce much more growth would be to help him to evaluate the feedback about his work objectively and to accept the judgments to the extent of their validity.

Hope and despair. These twin concepts merit extended discussion in this context of support and crisis utilization because they are so central to the helpee's recovery of his equilibrium, management of stress, and prevention of future crises. Korner (1970) has examined hope as a method of coping, a means of preventing crises, and as a route to healthy behavior. He points out that helpers appear to have mixed reactions about the values of hope. On the one hand, they believe that hope makes stress tolerable, but they are convinced also that it is foolhardy to rely on "false hopes." Few studies have been made of the helping functions of hope, but the general opinion among professional helpers seems to be that hope is more of a wishful panacea·than a dependable aid to solving personal problems. Perhaps it is the elusive quality of hope, the difficulty of defining it precisely, and its rich poetic language that limit its usefulness as a helping concept.

Instead of defining hope as expectations in the absence of verifiable facts it has been more fruitful to look at its opposite, hopelessness or despair. The anguish and pain of this condition are well known. Despair implies that the person has given up, that he has stopped trying to change the cause, that he feels dejected, and that he accepts the inevitability of the feared outcome. Korner indicates that "Hope induces a feeling of 'assumed certainty' that the dreaded event will not happen, that despair will not occur" (1970, p. 135). He goes on to say that "Hope is an assumption which is clung to because it is of fundamental importance to the life of the individual" (p. 136). When he becomes aware of these assumptions he may continue to use them as rationalizations to avoid despair, or he may see them as wishful thinking. In the latter case, he can manage them rationally in terms of his reality at that moment.

While hope remains primarily an emotional experience for the helpee, he can think and talk about it also. Thus, hope involves expectancies that are different from wishes for events that might occur. The central characteristic of hope for the helpee, therefore, is a ". . . quality of personal dependence on outcome . . ." (Korner 1970, p. 135), without building his actions " . . . on 'expectations' that it *must* happen in order to avoid undesirable and disagreeable dreaded outcomes" (Ibid., p. 135). The act of hoping is an act of faith with a feeling that a future event will ease his problems.

Some of the *values of hoping* are momentary comfort and relief from suffering. Hope mobilizes a reservoir of energy to meet present and future

sources of stress. For some it means psychological, and even physical, survival. Medical folklore is full of instances where hope sustained, and apparently facilitated recovery of the "incurably" ill.

A *limitation* of hope that the helper should watch for is the tendency for hope to become an escape from unpleasant realities. It is also easy for hopes to be transformed into more superficial, unrealistic wishes. The consequences of giving up wishes are not as great as losing hope. If the former happens, the helpee may be disappointed, but if hope diminishes, the person is vulnerable to doubt, or at worst, despair, insecurity, helplessness, and immobility.

Grief and loss. Grief is a normal emotional reaction to severe loss, usually of a significant person. An acute grief reaction may come considerably after the loss or traumatic event, or it may not come at all in the manner expected of normal people. Grief following bereavement may take a normal predictable course, called "grief work," or it may be expressed in distorted and dysfunctional behaviors. Lindemann (1944), who has written about acute grief most systematically, described the course of normal and morbid grief in a form useful for general helpers.

Normal grief is characterized by: (1) physical reactions—body distress in waves of twenty minutes to an hour, tightness and choking, sleeplessness, digestive disturbances, loss of appetite, sighing and shortness of breath, and weakness; (2) feelings of emptiness, tension, exhaustion, loss of warmth, and awareness of distance from people; (3) occasional preoccupation with images of the deceased; (4) occasional feelings of guilt over failure to do something, or exaggerations of self-accusations over small incidents; (5) change in activity patterns, restlessness, aimlessness, and searching for activity, yet lack in energy and motivation to follow through.

Morbid grief reactions are exaggerations of normal grief behaviors and may take the form of underreaction or delayed grief which may come years after the loss. Other forms are prolonged isolation, flights into expansiveness and well-being, unusually strong irritability or hostility toward friends and relatives, and prolonged depression. These reactions require specialized care, and the bereaved should be brought to the attention of a specialist, preferably a psychiatrist experienced in grief work, since medication is usually one of the supportive treatments utilized.

All available human resources need to be involved, even more than in normal grief reactions. Depending on the specific individual's wishes and background, the involvement of ministers with their traditional comforting rituals, reassurances, and relationships could help the person accept and relieve his suffering.

Lindemann (1944) described the "anticipatory grief reaction" which complicates relationships when prolonged absence, such as wartime, is present. Grief reactions sometimes take place after the separation and are worked through as if the absent person had died. When the absentee returns, as in the case of military personnel, both parties often are surprised at the emotional detachment of their reunion. The grief work had been carried out so effectively, probably as a protection in case of a death notice, that the spouse at home had no remaining feeling for the absentee. This kind of situation calls for a delicate rebuilding of relationships or facing the decision to remain separated.

The *normal course* of grief work consists of: (1) *accepting* the grief work process; (2) *expressing* the feelings of grief; (3) *dealing* with the memory of the deceased; (4) *readjusting* to the new environment without the deceased; (5) *building* new relationships. An important element in the helping process is to enable the bereaved to accept and work through this grief process.

Although this section has dealt with grief and loss in terms of bereavement and disaster, the principles apply to less intense reactions to loss, such as employment, property, or reputation. The strategies to follow are applicable to the full range of loss reactions from intense grief in bereavement to disappointment over a missed promotion. These strategies also apply to crises other than loss, such as conflict, arrest, and persecution.

Strategies for helping in crises

The following discussions pertain to general procedures for helping persons under stress or in a crisis condition. They are not intended, however, to be complete discussions of strategies for helping distressed people. It is not possible to offer panaceas or easy formulas because most sufferings of people, even of those experiencing sudden distress caused by uncontrolled events, evolve to very fundamental issues of life itself. In this sense it is very presumptuous to think of "helping," as we have considered it, much less try to write in a wise way about relief of human suffering. This discussion, therefore, is only suggestive and should encourage you to develop your own view of suffering and the human condition. You also should include in your study the numerous writings on these topics from religion, philosophy, and the behavioral sciences.

MULTIPLE IMPACT STRATEGY

Multiple impact strategy involves an intensive, as well as extensive, support effort, usually combined with an active behavior change program. Teams of agencies and specialists generally are involved, each making his impact at the appropriate time and sequence. Environmental, or milieu, support is combined with relationship support. An example is a family in crisis which is given a minimum of two days intensive round-the-clock attention. This treatment is given in a residential, or family service center setting rather than in an agency, office, or the family's home. Thus, the family has the advantage of a fresh environment, a total medical-social-psychological approach, and individualized help in the form of group and interview work. The assumptions underlying this strategy are that a family in crisis is a unit that must be helped as a unit, and that approaches to individual members would be ineffective. Total help in the early stages of a family crisis can be more effective than sporadic and progressive help later. The crisis can be used as a springboard for the family, or individuals therein, to mobilize their resources to deal with the crisis and to grow. In this process they learn how to prevent future crises.

This same multiple strategy is used with independent adults who face a crisis not involving a family. They may go to a retreat type of setting, or to a one-day program in a community mental health center and receive intensive attention from a variety of professional and nonprofessional helpers.

BUILDING AND MAINTAINING HOPE

Since hopelessness, despair and depression are such common components of stress and crisis, people depend heavily upon helpers to deal constructively with these conditions. Hope is the main antidote to despair as well as the source of relief from tension and frustration of unmet goals. It grants some satisfaction to the person to feel that the future may bring this relief. As Korner (1970) has indicated, hope includes strong emotional components akin to faith. People ". . . need them; they resist losing them; they fight to maintain them" (p. 136). To protect these fragile feelings, people develop a "rationalizing chain" which is ". . . formed from bits of reality accompanied by and held together by logic and reasoning" (p. 137). When stress or crises come along, however, they are managed usually by strengthening the weak links with rationalizations. These rationalizations may clash increasingly with the helpee's perceptions of reality, until either he tightens the rationalizing logic in his chain or he reverts to pure faith and feeling. Korner postulates a balanced condition, or "hope equation," between external sources of stress and a combination of faith and rationalizing which constitutes hope.

A first step in working with hope as a helping tool is to determine to what extent the nature and the degree of disturbance are in the feeling component, and to what extent in the rationalizing chain. If the feeling component is affected he may be depressed, but he is just as likely to have less visible feelings of hopelessness and the associated behaviors of passivity and detachment. In the case of sudden and severe loss, disorganization and dysfunction may be apparent.

After the helper has a better sense of what is going on in the helpee and how he is responding to the crisis, he can follow the general strategy of: (1) expression of feelings; (2) cognitive integration; (3) mobilization of resources; (4) action. The goal of this strategy is to get the helpee functioning minimally so that his deteriorative tendencies can be arrested and his strengths mobilized. The first step, then, is to get the helpee talking about his feelings and hopes. If he feels helplessness or numbness, for example, let him talk about them. While it may assist helpees facing less severe stress to move quickly to step 2—clarify their situations through rational discussion of their false logic and engage in problem solving activities—this approach generally is not useful when the stress is severe with accompanying feelings of intense hopelessness or helplessness. Ellis (1962) developed a step 2 cognitive approach that he labels "rational-emotive." He attempts to examine the helpee's self-defeating and catastrophic logic. The idea is to look critically at the messages the helpee gives himself about "being no good," "being a victim of circumstances," or "isn't it awful?" If you wish to understand this approach to changing a helpee's thinking about himself and his situation, look at Ellis' work listed among the suggested readings at the end of the chapter.

Most of the initial efforts toward helping the person build his hope structure are neither rational nor feeling oriented, but are based on action. Loosening the helpee from his lethargy and helpless feelings by encouraging activity aids his physical and mental well-being at this stage. Along with this approach should be a reasonable application of understanding skills to provide an awareness of emotional support. Simply being physically with the person as he talks about his feelings to a strong and understanding person has some supportive effect. If these initial approaches fail to alter his despairing mood or passivity pattern, or if his condition seems to be deteriorating into feeling and thought disorders (delusion, hallucination, paranoia, fixed and unreal ideas), emergency referral measures would be appropriate.

When the helpee has begun moving from his helpless feelings and passive behavior he can examine the "lost faith" and/or the missing links in his "rationalizing chain." The helper's main strategy at this stage is to continue his understanding support. He should watch for opportunities for reinforcing renewed hope, but he should also be aware of the

limitations of moving too close to approval of what the helpee is thinking and feeling. The choices about direction of the helpee's renewable
faith or reconstituted logic should be his, since these are value decisions.
What should be reinforced is the fact that he is making the effort of
renewing his hope.

The other option that the helpee faces at this juncture, besides re-
gaining hope, is to give up hoping and to face the situation or causes
of the crisis directly. He may construct a new hope structure better suited
to his needs for security and more functional for controlling his anxiety.
Regardless of which of the three options he chooses, the helpee needs
much supportive understanding at this stage. He needs encouragement
of efforts to reestablish his equilibrium and adaptive strength. When the
helpee reaches this stage of mastery of his crisis, he is in a position to
explore renewal steps described in the next strategy.

STRATEGY OF RENEWAL AND GROWTH

Renewal and growth strategy is aimed primarily at identification of
strengths in the person, helping him to bring these to awareness, and
then helping him develop a plan for releasing these growth potentials.
It is not a strategy designed for helpees still in a state of crisis, however.
This strategy requires skills in strength analysis and a whole array of
competencies for facilitating awareness. Much renewal work is done in
residential growth centers of which there are over 100 in the United
States alone. These centers are not associated with formal educational
structures, and they operate in a fairly unstructured fashion without
courses, grades, or credits. Much use is made of encounter groups, sensory awareness, gestalt integration, communications training, meditation,
and creative arts. A retreat type of setting facilitates concentration on
developing the new skills and experiences apart from the realities and
pressures of daily life. A laboratory approach is typical where the person
can try out new experiences in the protected atmosphere of the group or
growth center community without the risks inherent in real life settings.
The feedback under conditions of trust and safety is an invaluable contribution to personal growth. Participants establish their own growth
goals and use the resources of the center to reach them. The renewal
groups, for example, offer opportunities to reflect on values and purposes as well as to explore alternative life styles and to discover hidden
potentials.

For the helpee who has weathered a crisis and is at the stage of rebuilding, such renewal groups reinforce his hopes and strengths. He
experiences the warmth and support which come about from trusting
others who are themselves on the personal growth quest.

The limitations of this movement, however, are that its popularity has attracted many helping opportunists who are poorly qualified to facilitate such educational experiences. There are few effective ways to control abuses and destructive outcomes of such irresponsible growth efforts. Like so many potential aids, this growth movement has side effects and misuses, as does use of medicinal drugs. It is a case of "let the buyer beware"; so, it is essential to check carefully into the reputation of the growth center as well as into the backgrounds of the leaders before urging helpees to utilize this opportunity for renewal.

There is the consideration also that the leader may be highly skilled and may have an esteemed reputation, but still the experience could be inappropriate for this helpee at this time. All helpers, therefore, need to become familiar, preferably in first-hand experience, with the possibilities and limitations of various styles of renewal opportunities. Howard (1970) has reported on her year of explorations of these various growth experiences and cites her reactions to the centers, leaders, and styles of groups. Her book is a good starting place for those who are unfamiliar with growth groups.

THE CRISIS CENTER

For the helpee faced with continuing stress expressed as suicide attempts, drug abuse, or assault often needs the multiple approaches of a team of helpers. Most large communities now have such centers supported by community chests, private foundations, or public funds. Many are experimental efforts to meet community crises. They usually combine medical, psychological, and case work resources with peer helpers and volunteers. Examples are drug crisis clinics and suicide prevention centers. Even Travelers Aid, long concerned with people in distress, has been thrust increasingly into the crisis effort. Many centers operate telephone crisis lines that the person facing acute stress can call to get supportive help and referral information by phone.

THE HALFWAY HOUSE

The halfway house resource utilizes a strategy of facilitating transition from the crisis center or treatment facility to real life. Such houses are usually small home-like places with helping persons available in residence. The goal is to provide a semi-protected residential atmosphere where coping mechanisms and personality strengths can be developed prior to facing the demands of the real world. As the name implies, it is a facility, halfway between the protective institution, or clinic, and the normal community. Work-release programs from prisons have the same rationale.

THE TREATMENT CENTER

Treatment centers vary all the way from the total environmental control of the conventional hospital, day-care center, and community mental hygiene clinic to small home-like residential centers. An example is the Synanon-type center which focuses on drug rehabilitation performed by those who have been abusers of drugs but who have now adopted a different life style. They are also willing to assist others who want to change their style of coping with stress without the use of drugs.

Another example is the camp or farm for teenagers who cannot cope with the stress of family and community demands. The "Achievement Place" (Phillips 1971) in Kansas is an experimental program for teenage boys who are in trouble with the law and with their families. It is a residential environment that shapes behavior through a point system of rewards and support. A similar program, called "Learning House," is planned by Thoreson (1971) for children 3–12 who are having trouble in home or school. They are taken from their home environments for short periods to the special reward-controlled environment of the Learning House to relearn more adaptive forms of behavior.

THERAPEUTIC COUNSELING STRATEGY

Most of the strategies described above involve multiple approaches in environmentally controlled settings. Much of the helping process for people under stress or in crisis takes place in one-to-one interview formats, commonly labeled counseling. The usual strategy in counseling is to open the interview systematically with clarification of the reasons for the helpee's coming, establish mutual goals and responsibilities, then carry out a plan of action to reach the helpee's goals, and finally terminate the relationship. The counseling process varies according to the assumptions of the counselor about how behavior is changed and how personal problems are solved. In chapter 3, you will recall, examples of these varying styles were cited. Some counselors, such as Frankl (1965), use an existential framework which focuses on the meaning of existence. They see helping as a process of assisting the helpee's search for meaning in his existence and of putting tragedy and suffering in perspective. This "will to meaning" is not the same as faith or hope; it is a way of coping with the tension between what he is and what he could become. "Logotherapy," as Frankl describes his view, is a means for dealing with the meaninglessness so many persons feel about their lives. It focuses on changing the way man construes his existence as a way of confronting directly the anxiety of living. Corliss and Rabe (1969) describe and illustrate in more detail this style of helping people through crises.

Behavioral counseling approaches, on the other hand, focus on helping people to change the environments which shape their behavior. It is concerned with behavior that leads to the feelings of discomfort and the consequences of acts to relieve that distress. Comfort derives from feelings of mastery over self and environment. Behavioral counseling writers have had little to say about crises utilization, except in a general problem-solving framework.

CONSOLING STRATEGY

Consoling strategy is the traditional pastoral approach to comfort and crisis utilization. There is much more here than strong elements of therapeutic counseling. For those persons who respond to religious ritual, writings, and assurances of life after death, it is a powerful supportive strategy, particularly in times of bereavement. Childhood beliefs are reincorporated into the rational chain, and faith reestablishes hope. The person of the pastor has a supportive effect also through whatever associations of strength and protection are made to him. This may be some helpees' only means of managing grief so that they can move quickly through the grief process to new levels of growth and strength. Americans facing stress and crises still depend to a high degree upon religiously oriented helpers (Gurin et al., 1960).

Skills for comfort and crisis utilization

It is difficult to speak of special skills for creating conditions of comfort. As indicated earlier in the chapter, comfort is due largely to the personal qualities transmitted by the helper. Just being with the helpee in an attentive way during periods of stress is comforting. Thus, almost all the skills for understanding also convey support and result in comfort. Listening to the helpee ventilate his feelings, for example, has a powerfully supportive effect. Similarly the skills for action to be described in the next chapter have implications for helping the person move from the passivity, so often characteristic of the person in crisis, to action in building new relationships and planning for the future. The following skills can be used as supplements for those described earlier to produce conditions of comfort and to make use of the growth potential of crises.

CONTACTING SKILLS

Chapter 5 described *eye contact* as an essential ingredient in attending to the helpee. This nonphysical contact reassures the helpee that the helper is with him. Physical *touch* is another form of contact that has powerful comforting qualities. We all know this from our experiences with our families and friends. Among helpers, however, the question of touching helpees is very controversial. Putting a hand on a pupil's shoulder as a gesture of support and perhaps affection by teachers is considered inappropriate by many helpers and parents. We in America seem to have strong touch taboos not present in many other societies. Even though we recognize the power of touch to comfort, and even though many helpers favor its use, they must regard touch as a high risk method at the present time. The decision to touch depends on the context and structure of the helping relationship. Touching is more permissible in the informal helping situation because it is more akin to friendship where touching is encouraged.

Touch should be used with discretion, after consideration of agency policy, and the age and sex of the helpee. Holding a helpee's hand, or putting a firm hand on his arm or shoulder while he is struggling with a painful feeling can be most helpful to comfort or to facilitate further exploration. Embracing or sitting on laps, for example, would be a high risk behavior considering present mores; but, again, under present circumstances of rapid cultural change it might be the appropriate thing to do for the helpee's benefit. When using physical contact it is important that the helper have a high degree of awareness of his own needs for contact and should be sufficiently in touch with his own feelings so he can be perceptive about the helpee's needs and reactions to his contacting skills. In other words, the foremost question to be answered is, "Whose needs are being served?" We should be alert, for example, to helpees whose experiences with the opposite sex and close human relationships generally have been so restricted that they react with intense anxiety to any kind of physical contact. There are reported instances where helper contact has been misinterpreted to the point where accusations of seduction or molestation have been made. Some of these claims were probably justified as unethical behavior, but some were undoubtedly misjudgments of the helper about the nature of the state of trust and mutual acceptance present. This contact issue must be decided finally on the bases of: (1) the good judgment of the helper about the needs of this helpee; (2) the helper's awareness of his own needs and ethics; (3) what is likely to be most helpful within the helper's rationale of helping; and (4) what risks the helper is willing to take, all factors considered (agency policy, local custom, age, sex, and attitude of helpee, professional ethics).

REASSURING SKILLS

Reassurance is a method of verbally assuring the helpee about the consequences of his actions or feelings. It acts as a kind of reward since it reduces stress and builds confidence, and also builds expectancies of future rewards. Examples of reassuring types of comments and suggestions are, "You are competent." "You can be reasonable." "You can solve your problem." "You can feel better." The goals of using reassurance are to increase the helpee's confidence, mobilize his strengths, reduce his anxiety to optimum working levels, or reinforce a desired behavior.

One reassuring skill is *expressing approval* of a helpee's statement. You say, for example, "That sounds to me like a good idea—very thoughtful." It is a process of agreeing with the helpee and of course, reinforcing his expression. One paradoxical limitation of reassurance is that it tends to fix the stated idea; the helpee, as a consequence, is less likely to change that idea or behavior.

A second reassuring skill is *predicting outcomes*. The helper says, for example, "You have been exploring your feelings pretty intensively today. You really have been spilling it out the last few minutes and now we have to go. You'll probably find yourself a bit moody the next couple of days; but this happens frequently, so don't worry about it." Another example is, "You have had a tough adjustment to face with your father's death, and it will probably continue to be rough for awhile; but you will be able to handle it all right."

A third use of reassuring skill is *factual assurance*. Telling the helpee that his problem has a solution, that people with his kind of difficulty make it, or that annoying symptoms disappear at fairly predictable times, enables him to tolerate the momentary stress. Reassurance can be given at an even more specific factual level, such as, assuring him that there are known steps to formulate sound career plans or of improving study performance.

Some of the *limitations* and *cautions* in using reassurance are: (1) It is easy to use, so there is a temptation to *overuse* it. (2) It may cause *hostility* in the helpee who may feel the true nature of some serious condition was concealed or minimized. He may feel that the helper is *minimizing* the seriousness of his feelings by remarks that indicate that "everything will come out all right," or "it isn't as bad as you think it is." (3) Reassurance efforts come across so often as insincere *sympathy*, which may jeopardize the whole helping relationship. (4) *Dependency* is often encouraged by use of reassurance because the person needs periodic doses, which then act as a mechanism for avoiding change in his behavior. (5) If the reassurance is interpreted as agreement, the helpee may feel *trapped* in his present thinking and action.

In summary, guidelines for reassurance are:

1. Depend mainly on the positive quality of the relationship for supportive reassurance rather than relying on verbal forms of assurance.
2. Use verbal reassurance mainly to reduce distress through facts and predictions.
3. Use reassurance sparingly as a reinforcing agent to encourage continuing behaviors.

RELAXING SKILLS

Stress is usually accompanied by physical tension. One of the most direct forms of inducing comfort is to work directly on muscle tension. There are a number of styles of inducing relaxation through direct suggestion. Jacobson (1938) has a form of progressive relaxation that systematically induces relaxation in large muscle groups by alternating the tensing and releasing of these muscles. Some practitioners have put their induction methods on tape; Lazarus' (1971) recording is an example. Inducing relaxation is a simple skill to learn and it has few hazards. Occasionally, hypersuggestible persons appear to go into a kind of hypnotic state which may become a problem for the beginning helper. Simply telling the helpee that when you finish counting to five he will wake up usually is sufficient.

Other ways to induce relaxation are simple focusing on breathing, even counting slowly on inhaling and slowly on exhaling. One limitation in such prolonged efforts is a condition called "hyperventilation" where the person may feel momentarily dizzy or faint after breathing too deeply. Certain body positions, such as those advocated in Yoga, induce relaxation also. Vocalizations, such as chants, sighing deeply, and repeating expansive sounds, such as "a-ohm," help some people to relax. States of awareness, or consciousness, advocated by Zen practitioners also promote ease and physical relaxation. Hot baths with fast moving water have been used for millenia to induce relaxation. Since a detailed discussion of relaxation methods is beyond the scope of this chapter, the serious helper who desires to use these skills in his helping relationships should read some of the basic works on physical relaxation and the Eastern Zen and Yoga writers on awareness and meditation.

The *uses* of relaxation skills are varied. They may be used as a primary method to produce relief from tension precipitated by stressful conditions. The helpee frequently reacts with gratitude at the rapidity of relief which is afforded, and thus feels more confidence in your ability to help him. Relaxation methods can be applied when you wish to reduce his anxiety and physical tension to sufficiently tolerable limits so that verbal skills can be utilized for understanding, comfort, or action. Relaxation methods also are part of the sequence of systematic desensitization, a method for changing behavior to be described in the next chapter.

Guidelines on relaxing skills are:

1. Learn a verbally-induced relaxation method that is comfortable for you.
2. Learn the importance of focusing on breathing as a quick relaxation method.
3. Become familiar with various psychological forms of relaxation as practiced by Eastern mystics, as an adjunct to your physical relaxation methods.

CENTERING SKILLS CLUSTER

Development of centering comfort skills assumes that the helper regards the human personality as something beyond a collection of its components. Centering is a process of getting "in touch" and then "in tune" with one's person, or total self. Centering results in awareness of peace, harmony, unity, and strength. There are a variety of helper styles of centering. One is a progressive awareness process where the helper tells the helpee to close his eyes, get comfortable, and breath slowly and deeply. Then he goes through a few verbal suggestions to guide his awareness to his center of being. Say, for example, "Your body is part of you . . . , but your body is not the total you; what else is there? You have feelings; they are part of you . . . , but your feelings are not the total you. What else is there? You are a thinking being; you have ideas . . . , but your thoughts are not the total you. You have a center where all of these parts of you come together, a center of your being where you experience peace, wholeness, strength . . . ; this center is an important part of you . . . ."

The brief illustration above was presented to help you understand centering methods. They are used to help a person who feels out of tune, or even at "war" with himself. The parts of him are working at cross purposes and consuming enormous amounts of energy. His body, for example, may be out of phase with his thoughts. The aim is to promote an awareness of smoothness and unity as a means toward comfort. The method also is designed to get the parts back into some kind of balance. Some helpees, for example, seem to have exaggerated awareness and valuing of their bodies to the exclusion of other phases of existence. It is very comforting in crisis situations, also, for helpees to realize the center of their being as a place where they can find peace and strength. This experience of centering has great survival value for our society.

Corliss and Rabe (1969) speak of two modes of being, peripheral and central. The person existing at the peripheral level is concerned with doing, with changing the physical world. The center is more an existence in fantasy, the "as if" world, a place of quietude and receptivity. One of the key problems of living is maintaining an effective balance between these two modes of existence.

Strength analysis is also a method of centering, although it operates more as a descriptive device to build strength and confidence. It is applicable to nonstress situations as well and is a form of building strength to utilize future crises constructively. It is the simple exercise of asking the helpee to focus on his strong points and to list them out loud. It may only be three or four but they are usually sufficient to start the helpee's thinking of his positive strengths. In periods of stress the usual tendency is to focus on weak and negative personal qualities and to exaggerate them. Self-abnegation and criticism often accompany depressed moods. This method of strength analysis is *not* a method of reassuring the person that he is strong and capable or suggesting that "Every day in every way, I'm getting better and better." The list of strengths, with specific examples, comes from the helpee.

Reviewing growth experiences is a method of asking the helpee to focus upon pleasant or unpleasant experiences (the more recent, the better) that have had a profoundly positive effect on his growth. This is often interpreted to mean traumatic events that have had a frustrating or negative effect. These may be dealt with productively at another time. The helpee's focus must be on events that had positive outcomes. This process leads to reexperiencing feelings long outside of his awareness. The effect is strengthening the helpee's image of himself as a capable person with the strength to meet stress and crisis. He can point to specific instances where he has done so in the past.

Reviewing peak experiences has an effect similar to the growth experience analysis above. In chapter 1, we discussed Maslow's term "peak experience" to mean those life experiences, usually short and infrequent, when the person is aware of intense pleasure, exhilaration, joy, and fulfillment. Recalling and focusing on such experiences can be rewarding in terms of comfort and satisfaction.

CRISIS INTERVENING SKILLS

Crisis intervening skills are a cluster of skills, most of which have been described in other contexts. These skills induce comfort through support and understanding, or through altering the helpee's response by a change in his environment. Those skills which were cited as building hope, contact through touching, and comfort through empathic listening apply to crisis situations. Supportive actions through changed living arrangements and sedative drugs are additional methods used by specialists to alter the helpee's environment. The presence of a warm and understanding person, not involved with the crisis himself, is very supportive in crises. Referral methods for special forms of help (described below) are part of the crisis intervention cluster also.

REFERRING SKILLS

There are times when even the most skilled and confident helpers admit frustration and defeat in dealing with persons in crisis. Referral is one approach where the helpee can have a fresh start. For the beginning helper, referral is a common method of managing crisis conditions in helpees. This seems so obvious, but the reason for considering referral as a special helping skill is that there are some specific ways of referring to make it effective. Some of the principles of referral are:

1. Know community resources for different kinds of services.
2. Explore the helpee's readiness for referral. Has he expressed interest in specialized help? Is he afraid of seeing a "shrink"? Do we frighten him with implications of the severity of his problem, such as the inflection we give to, "You had better see a psychiatrist!"?
3. Be direct and honest about your observations of his behavior which led to your suggested referral. Be honest also about your own limitations. If after working with him for awhile, you feel that it would be in his best interest to receive more intensive help from a specialist, you might say something like, "Let's explore what other possible resources would be available for help with this question." This illustrative statement does not imply he is too disturbed or confused for you to handle and therefore he must be in *really* bad shape.
4. It is usually desirable to discuss the possibility of referral with the referral agency before the problem becomes urgent.
5. Determine what other persons have had contact with this helpee and confer with them before suggesting further steps.

6. If the helpee is a minor it is wise to inform the parents of your recommendations and obtain their consent and cooperation.

7. Be fair in explaining the services of a referral agency by citing the possibilities and the limitations of that agency. Do not imply that miracles can be performed there.

8. Let the helpee or his parent make their own appointments for the new service, although sometimes supportive services like offering transportation would be facilitative.

9. Do not release information to any referral source without written permission from the helpee or his parents in the form of a signed release.

10. If you have been having the primary helping relationship with him, it is only ethical to maintain that relationship until the referral is complete and a new relationship is begun.

Outcomes you should expect from studying this chapter

Now that you have studied this chapter you can: (1) describe and illustrate the terms stress, crisis, support, hope, and grief; (2) describe and illustrate eight helping strategies for dealing with stress and crisis; (3) list three skills from the chapter on understanding which have supportive effects also; (4) describe two arguments for and against contacting, reassuring, and relaxing skills; (5) list ten principles for referral of helpees to other persons or agencies. The final outcome to be expected is your ability to apply these methods and principles such that helpees feel and act in ways that indicate confidence and comfort.

Suggestions for further study

Brammer, L., and Shostrom, E. *Therapeutic Psychology.* 2nd ed. Englewood Cliffs, N.J.: Prentice-Hall, 1968. (Ch. 6 on support functions, Ch. 7 on reassurance methods, and Ch. 15 on value problems.)

Corliss, R., and Rabe, P. *Psychotherapy from the Center: A Humanistic View of Change and Growth.* Scranton, Pa.: International Textbook, 1969. (An existential view of counseling strategy.)

Ellis, A. *Reason and Emotion in Psychotherapy.* New York: Lyle Stewart, 1962. (A method of helping people in crisis look at their illogical thinking.)

Farber, M. *A Theory of Suicide.* New York: Funk & Wagnalls, 1968. (An analysis of the experience of suicide prevention centers.)

Feifel, H. *The Meaning of Death.* New York: McGraw-Hill, 1959. (A psychological approach to death and dying.)

Gardner, J. *Self-renewal.* New York: Harper & Row, 1963. (A short essay on the necessity for renewing individuals and changing institutions.)

HOWARD, J. *Please Touch.* New York: McGraw-Hill, 1970. (A newswoman's report of a year in various growth centers.)

KUBLER-ROSS, E. *On Death and Dying.* New York: Crowell Collier and Macmillan, 1969. (Psychological issues and methods for dealing with death.)

LESTER, G., and LESTER, D. *Suicide: The Gamble with Death.* Englewood Cliffs, N.J.: Prentice-Hall, 1971. (A broad behavioral science study of suicide.)

LINDEMANN, E. "Symptomatology and management of acute grief." *American Journal of Psychiatry* 101 (1944); 7-21. Reprinted in Parad, H. *Crisis Intervention: Selected Readings,* Ch. 1. (Practical suggestions for managing extreme loss reactions.)

MARIN, P., and COHEN, A. *Understanding Drug Use.* New York: Harper & Row, 1971. (An adult's guide to drugs and the young.)

PARAD, H. *Crisis Intervention: Selected Readings.* New York: Family Service Association of America, 1965. (A collection of reprints on grief, family crises, maternal reactions, school entry, relocation, illness, and psychiatric crises.)

8 | *Helping skills for positive action*

People come to helpers mainly because they are unhappy about some aspect of their behavior. Although they do not always state their goal as wanting to change a specific behavior, like shyness, they soon see that it is their actions that must be the ultimate focus of their attention. Essentially, all helping is aimed toward action outcomes of some kind. If specific actions are involved, the process is described usually as behavior modification. This process of changing behavior applies not only to observable actions but also to covert or internal behavior. Examples are how the person thinks of himself, how he feels about another person, or how he views his world. These are determined from self-reports of the person himself, but we look for specific actions to verify his verbal statements about his internal state. For example, we look for positive self-descriptions if he feels good about himself. We also make inferences about what is going on in his thinking and feeling by observing his actions. An example is the degree of assertive social behavior exhibited by a helpee as an index of how confident he feels about himself when he is around others.

A positive action approach gives the helper specific evidence that he has been helpful to the extent that the helpee has reached his goals.

There is much discussion about "accountability" in all helping agencies. This means that you assume a large share of responsibility as the helper to meet specific behavioral outcomes of the helping process. It means that you look for evidence that the helpee is achieving the goals determined in the early stages of the helping process described in chapter 4. When we talk about an action program in an accountability framework, it assumes that the helpee was involved extensively in both establishing and assessing the objectives.

Positive action refers to two types of processes which will form the remaining content of this chapter. One is a problem-solving and decision-making cluster of processes and skills. The other cluster of skills is aimed at changing specific kinds of behaviors usually expressed as the acquisition of a skill rather than the removal of a deficiency. Some examples of the kinds of concerns brought to helpers which have specific skill involvement are improving study skills, acquiring social skills, developing more assertive behaviors, and diminishing unnecessary fears. Essentially, the helper is in the position of a teacher of skills for solving problems, changing behavior, and achieving higher levels of functioning.

There are practically unlimited possibilities for improving human capacities. Numerous writers on the human potential estimate that we use about ten percent of our potentialities. Studies underway on control of body functions, particularly brain powers, will open vast reservoirs of energy and action potential. Various methods of monitoring our own behavior, controlling negative thoughts, improving self-images. and altering our consciousness at will are not too far off. Helpers skilled in teaching others how to manage their own behavior through knowledge of behavior-changing and problem-solving skills will have a powerful helping resource to draw upon.

Persons both in and out of the helping framework have mixed feelings, sometimes even outright rejection, of the behavior modification approach. They equate it to "brainwashing," at worst, and to "salvation of society" at the optimistic end of the spectrum. These methods *are* powerful techniques for changing behavior which can be misapplied by unscrupulous people. This is a problem analogous to using chemicals to alter behavior for better or for worse. These behavior changing methods can enhance a helpee's freedom in many ways by expanding his options for choice. He can acquire a wider response repertoire; he can determine his own goals; and he can have something to say about the methods used to achieve those goals. So, the issue is not the processes and skills that have good or evil in themselves, but it is the ethical or unethical manner in which they are used. The basic problem is not *whether* the helpee's behavior will be controlled, but *by whom* and *for whose benefit.* Behavior modification is a technology, not an ethical system.

Outcomes expected from studying this chapter

The purpose of this chapter is to examine the processes and skills that will accomplish the helping functions described above. The focus is on acting and changing externally observable behavior, whereas the preceding two chapters emphasized more subtle changes in social attitude, self-regard, and perception of life circumstances. As a result of studying this chapter you will have competencies to: (1) describe the steps in a problem-solving and decision-making model of helping; (2) apply relevant skills in appropriate sequences; (3) describe and illustrate skills for changing behavior such as modeling, contracting, rewarding, extinguishing, desensitizing, and aversion-controlling.

Although it is unrealistic to expect to apply these skills after reading about them, it is reasonable for you to expect to try them out with understanding and to evaluate your success with them. Since you will have specific kinds of outcomes to observe, these skills should be easier to evaluate than those described in previous chapters. A note of caution, though: These behavior modification skills appear deceptively simple to apply, yet they require practice and feedback from those who are specialized in behavior modification methods. After you study the methods here and in the suggested readings, find a setting in which you can try these skills under supervision of a behavioral change specialist.

Characteristics and assumptions of the action approach to helping

CHARACTERISTICS

The main focus in the action approach is changing *specific helpee behaviors,* whereas the focus in the two preceding chapters has been on general goals and on changing perceptions and feelings as intermediate goals. Whereas change in behavior is the ultimate standard for judging success of all helping styles, the action approach places special stress on helpee behavioral outcomes. Action methods are characterized by an objective empirical approach to helpee goals and environmental change.

Action approaches come under the helping strategy called behavioral counseling. The principal characteristics of this strategy are: (1) careful assesment of the helpee's problem behavior and conditions that maintain that behavior; (2) agreement on precise *goals* for new behaviors; (3) application of mainly *change skills* described below but utilization of all helping skills; (4) evaluation of *outcomes* in relation to goals; (5) *feedback* information to improve the process. Behavioral counseling strategists stress the importance of learning problem-solving methods so that self-directed action can take place in everyday problems situations.

Behavioral types of helpers look at the helpee's present behavior and the complex environment in which it takes place. Thus, the helper takes minimum notice of psychological traits and problems. Some behavioral helpers, especially in working with children, get a baseline count of the child's undesirable and desirable behaviors before doing anything else. This gives them a basis for judging the effectiveness of the help in terms of decreases of undesirable and increases in desirable behavior.

ASSUMPTIONS

Behavior is the result of interactive external environmental forces and internal heredity forces. Continued responses are the result of learning by imitation and reward. Behavior is mediated somewhat by thinking processes, also, and is not only an automatic response to a rewarding environment. Social learning is a function of the interaction between the person's early behavior patterns and controlling environmental social conditions. The basic framework for action helping methods is the social learning approach described by Bandura (1969). Although the environment has profound impact on the person's behavior, sometimes his behavior also alters the social environment considerably.

The use of behavior change methods assumes that the helpee comes for expert help in changing a specific behavior and is not seeking a supportive friendly relationship or an examination of his value commitment. These latter kinds of help, covered in previous chapters, are not suited to the behavior technology approaches described below.

IMPLICATIONS

Some implications of the action approach for the helping process are that helper and helpee try to establish goals, find solutions, and make plans together. As a helper, you will use a variety of methods to help the helpee achieve his specific goals. You will be responsible to observe what is happening at all times so that you can define in concrete ways what progress, if any, the two of you are making toward the helpee's goals. While you will trust your judgment and feelings about what is going on, you will look for specific outcomes to check your hunches. By being very specific with the helpee about concrete outcomes, you keep vagueness and mysticism out of the helping process. You say, for example, "I agreed to work with you, but you need to do some work outside of our talk sessions because what you do out there, specifically, where you live, is the important payoff of our work here. We will be talking about very concrete things you can do to help your situation out there, and we will want to look occasionally at the progress we are making."

This action approach is not an emotionally sterile and strictly rational procedure, as is often claimed. Action methods work very effectively in a relationship characterized by the facilitative conditions described in chapter 2. Mickelson and Stevic (1971) found that behaviorally oriented counselors with high warmth, empathy, and genuineness were more effective in generating information seeking responses in their helpees than those behavioral counselors rated low on facilitative conditions.

Problems and goals

Since action outcomes are our concern, it is very important to identify specific problems and translate those problems into precise goals. Helpees seldom come with neatly stated problems. They are usually expressed in vague feelings of confusion, dissatisfaction, or distress. Often complaints are focused on another person or institution. Thus, the helper begins, as in other styles of helping, with listening for understanding. He tries to communicate this understanding, and often this is enough for the helpee to feel understood and comforted. If the helper's listening reveals helpee needs for *acting* differently, however, another strategy is needed. As he listens the helper is gaining information about the specifics in the helpee's life, how he looks at himself and others, what he wants, and what his environment is like. From these data about helpee's initial complaints and feelings, the helper and helpee together *describe* how he *acts now* and how he would *like to act*. Thus, *goals* are formulated toward which he can work with some help from the helper in the form of suggested methods. Goals, according to Krumboltz (1966) must meet three criteria: (1) the goals are desired by the helpee and tailored to him; (2) the helper is willing to help him work toward the goal; (3) attainment of the goal is observable and assessable. Krumboltz emphasizes that general goals, such as "self-understanding" and "self-actualization," are accepted by almost everyone, but to be useful in an action approach they must be stated in the unique and specific language of the helpee. An example of such a specific action goal is, "I want to avoid crying every time I am criticized." This goal implies that the helpee will understand why he cries, but it goes beyond understanding and relief of distress to the action of changing crying behavior.

Krumboltz' second criterion, willingness of the helper, is significant because the goals of the helpee must fit the ethical, legal, and competency requirements of the helper. For example, it would not be appropriate for a helper to be a party to a helpee's scheme to cheat on an examination or take advantage of a weaker person, even though it were very important to the helpee to do so. The helper should always have the option of refusing help if he feels the goals are questionable.

DIFFICULTIES IN STATING GOALS

Changing helpee problems into specific goals with observable outcomes is one of the principal difficulties in the action approach. Some of the difficulties cited by Krumboltz and Thoreson (1969) are as follows.

1. It is important to determine who the helpee is. This problem was discussed in chapter 4 under the second process stage—clarification. The following brief example will illustrate the problem in this special context. If a parent refers a child for counseling, it is easy to be confused about who needs help—the parent or the child. The helpee is defined as the person who brings the problem to the helper, since for the time being, at least, he "owns" the problem. Although the helper may understand the plight of the person who is trying to get another person in for help, sometimes he has to say firmly, "Let's discuss how I might help you deal with this person so you can help him to change his behavior." You, as a helper, may still want to see the other person, but at least there is a helping partnership established with the referring person so you are not carrying the full responsibility for a most difficult helping situation.

2. The helpee *expresses his problem as a feeling* such as, "I am miserable . . . I am lonely . . . I am frustrated." After applying the skills for understanding to help clarify the feeling statements, Krumboltz and Thoreson suggest a further approach: Ask the helpee, "What could you *do* to make yourself wanted, attractive, or loved by other persons?" The assumption here is that the helpee needs to take some kind of action that is counter to the feeling expressed and that will gain him the response he wants—love, respect, or money, for example. This step may mean acquiring a new competency.

Another problem faced by helpers is the person with high aspirations and unrealistic standards. He continually compares himself to others of extraordinary competence. Furthermore, he assumes his feelings of incompetence or loneliness are unique to him because we seldom share these feelings and have little basis for judging the realism of our feelings. Help in this situation consists mainly of receiving accurate information about others' feelings, making realistic plans for achievement, and accepting the reality of the frustration and disillusionment.

3. *Lack of a goal* and not knowing his own desires can be a source of difficulty for the helpee. Krumboltz and Thoreson point out that such helpees must come to realize that values and goals are not discovered but are created by the person for himself. Thus, the most helpful thing one can do with such "purposeless and alienated" people is to encourage them to construct goals for *their* lives or to adopt goals of other groups—religious, political, social, service—to give purpose to their existence. Most people need some large purpose or cause to give meaning and zest to their lives. The general helping strategy is to engage them in an active, exploratory process where they try on different goals and organizational identities until they find some that match their vaguely defined desires.

4. Desired *goals may be inappropriate*. A helpee may want to do something that, in your opinion, is against his best interests. If we really believe that he must make his own decisions, the most we can do is offer our opinions as an additional bit of information he can consider. Hopefully, that opinion is solicited. Sometimes helpees don't know why their behavior is disliked or unacceptable. They often give the helper a biased view so he really cannot get a clear idea of the helpee's problem. An example is the teenager who says others do not like him and he cannot tell why. The general helping strategy is to encourage him to make note of what he is doing to make himself unwanted and to set goals for trying new behaviors that make him more attractive to others.

5. *Choice conflict* is another situation difficult to translate into a behavioral goal. A common condition brought to helpers is one in which all the choices are unacceptable or unattainable. An example is the couple who want separation to resolve their conflict, yet do not want the financial problems associated with a divorce. The general helping strategy is to decide whether the helpee needs to learn problem-solving skills or to explore the full range of alternatives. In any case, the helper must confront the helpee with the necessity to pin down a goal such as exploring all the possible consequences of each choice facing him.

6. Sometimes helpees have *no real problem,* but just want to talk. They do not want an action goal to work toward. The helper then

must decide if he wants to spend his time in this manner or suggest that the helpee find someone else to "rap" with.

MOVING BEYOND GOALS

We have been discussing some of the difficulties of translating problems into specific goal statements which make sense to the helpee. Once the goals have been agreed upon, the skill of contracting is brought to bear on the question of how, when, and by whom the goal-seeking efforts will be initiated and maintained. The process of comparing results against the goals is a continuous one, so the helper knows when he is succeeding. If the helpee is not moving toward the mutually determined goals at a reasonable rate, a diagnostic inquiry must be started to answer the question, "Why not?" Then a corrective procedure can be instituted.

Finally, the evaluation of the process is undertaken to see what can be learned that will make helping for action strategies more successful. Evaluation of helpee outcomes against specific goals for action also makes accountability for performing the helping tasks much easier to demonstrate. Those helpers working in an agency context are finding this evaluative function a political necessity for survival as well as a continuing professional obligation.

The following is a summary of key characteristics of helping for action:

1. The helper uses listening and reflecting skills to *discover central problems* and assess his situation.
2. The helper assists the helpee to state his problem(s) in *behavioral terms* as a goal(s) to be achieved.
3. The helper and helpee agree on the *priority of problems* to be solved and acceptable levels of success.
4. The helper utilizes his *full range of skills* to work toward helpee goals.
5. The helpee gives evidence that he is *aware of the consequences* of each action alternative.
6. The process is *monitored* continuously. The helper and helpee agree on *evaluation* of progress and any *changes in strategy* to be instituted.
7. The helper and helpee plan the *transition* from learning coping skills to maintaining new behaviors in their natural setting without the helping relationship.
8. The helper and helpee decide if the *primary goal* and subgoals have been reached and if the helpee has learned the personal problem-solving process.

9. The entire helping process is *evaluated* and *examined for learnings* to be applied in future helping relationships.

The action approach is well-suited to two general kinds of helping—problem-solving and changing or adding specific behaviors. First we will consider a decision-making and problem-solving model with related skills. Then, we will look at some skill clusters helpful in changing specific behaviors.

Problem-solving and decision-making

A significant number of helpee concerns can be translated into problems to be solved or decisions to be made among two or more alternatives. Common life decisions such as, "What career should I plan for," "What changes should I make in my life?" "Should I marry this person?" "Should I stay here or take this new job offer?" are suited to this problem-solving strategy of helping. The following discussion is based on the assumption that decision-making involves skills that can be learned and applied in many contexts.

A second important helper consideration is, "How can I teach the helpee to solve his own problems?" We are not helping him very much if we provide a temporary process for the helpee to solve an immediate problem, and then he continues to seek out helpers every time he faces a new problem. One strategy for learning this process is direct instruction in problem-solving procedure. Another strategy is simulation—an artificial or game approach similar to the real life situation. The helpee can make choices and experience consequences vicariously without dire results. An example is the "Career Game" by Varenhorst (1969). For helpees planning a career this is a way of providing simulated decision-making conditions. A fictitious person making career choices is presented. The helpees work in teams deciding how that person will spend his time over eight years. Decisions are interdependent and scoring is based on probability tables that reflect job, education, and marriage opportunities in American culture. Many decisions are involved and consequences are known immediately to the teams so the helpee players can learn the problem-solving process from early feedback.

THE PROBLEM-SOLVING PROCESS

The steps below follow general problem-solving sequences and are applied to many problems, but most of the illustrations are in the area of educational and career planning as exemplified by Brammer and

Shostrom (1968) and Krumboltz and Sheppard (1969). These general steps are:

1. Establish a *relationship* and get the helpee *involved*. Helpee must be interested in the process and have hope that they have the power to make decisions that will influence their lives profoundly.
2. State and clarify the *problem* and determine *goals*. This step is a special application of the goal-setting process described in the preceding section.
3. Determine and explore *alternatives* to the mere apparent solutions.
4. Gather relevant *information*. This may take the form of active seeking and reading by the helpee, statements of fact by the helper, simulation games, films, or tests.
5. Explore *implications* of information and *consequences* of the alternatives.
6. Clarify *values* that underly personal choices. Helpees must know what they desire and the order in which they value those desires. The helper leads the helpee into exploration of his interests, competencies, family circumstances, social expectations, and realities.
7. *Re-examine the goals,* alternative choices, risks, and consequences. A final check on understanding the information and implications is made before the final decision.
8. *Decide* on one of the alternatives and formulate a *plan* for or course of action implementing that decision.
9. *Generalize* the process to new life situations.
10. *Try out* the plan for implementing the decision with periodic *re-evaluation* in light of new information and changing circumstances.

Most people, particularly young ones, have limited life experiences in making decisions and are generally unfamiliar with this rational process. Therefore, many helpees must be taught this process through problem-solving interviews, direct trial-and-error experiences, and through limitations, such as "Career Games," "Marriage Games," and "War Games." Young helpees often ask outright, "What shall I do?" "What course should I take?" "Should I try drugs?" "What career should I choose?" "What college should I apply to?" Instead of giving advice or opinions it is preferable to say, "I can't tell you because I don't know what is best for you; but I can help you decide for yourself what to do. Would you like to learn how?" There is abundant evidence in guidance studies that school-age youth make poor quality decisions about many areas of their lives. If you, as a helper, are faced with helping youth to make plans for the future, it would be time well spent to delve more deeply into the special areas of knowledge required to apply the above decision-making model to educational, vocational, and social planning. An illustrative program designed for students from grades seven through nine is described by Miller and Gelatt (1971). They have constructed a program that includes helping young students to: (1) identify critical decision points; (2) recognize and clarify personal values; (3) identify alternatives and create new ones; (4) seek, evaluate and utilize information; (5) take risks; and (6) develop strategies for decision-making.

Magoon (1969) describes a procedure for decision-making with adults called "Effective Problem Solving." It is a thirteen part procedure for teaching college students with educational-vocational planning problems how to solve problems by themselves, at their own pace, under monitoring by a counselor. Magoon's method is another illustration of teaching the problem-solving process to helpees. His model and format is adaptable to many problem-solving situations where group and independent study approaches rather than individual counseling are indicated.

Decisions in the areas of interpersonal problems, such as sexual behavior involving previously learned response patterns, are more complicated. Solutions to these problems involve relearning methods as well as rational problem-solving described above. Adult helpees who face difficult choices, such as what to do with rebellious children, dependent relatives, errant spouses, or changes of work locale must be taught this same problem-solving process as a substitute for acting on impulses, stereotypes, or advice.

SKILLS REQUIRED IN PROBLEM SOLVING

Most problem-solving skills are combinations of those described in other contexts: problem identification, goal setting, informing, interpreting, diagnosing, and evaluating feedback. There is a skill applicable to Step 3, generating and weighing alternatives, called "force field" analysis. This skill utilizes physics concepts of fields of force and polarized valences. It is a method of comparing personal and social forces which are propelling the helpee toward his goal and distracting him from it at the same time. Force field skills are applicable to many kinds of decision-making situations. The helpee's goal is stated briefly at the top of Figure 8, and the direction of solution is indicated by an arrow. The forces pushing him toward his alternative goal (in this simple illustration, to reduce weight by three pounds a week for six weeks) are indicated by a + sign, and those working against him by a − sign. After listing the + and − forces, he can see more clearly where he is in relation to the feasibility of his goal. He then can rank the forces on their strength by rating each from 1 to 3. Now the helpee can decide on a strategy of strengthening the + forces or weakening the − forces. If it is a conflict of choice problem, each alternative goal can be analyzed and then compared. You can see, for example, how useful such a model would be when helping a youth to decide whether or not to become involved with hard drugs.

FIGURE 8.   Illustration of force field analysis.

GOAL: Reducing weight by three pounds a week for six weeks. ⟶

+	Rank	−	Rank
Spouse likes me thinner	1	Like rich food	3
Better for my health	2	Dislike diets and diet foods	1
Live longer	3	Lack knowledge of low calorie foods	2
Clothes will fit better	1	Will smoke instead of eat	2
Less fatigue	3	Three pounds seems too much in a week	1

Balance
Point for
Forces

The following list is a summary of problem-solving steps:

1. *Involve* the helpee.
2. State the *problem,* assess the *setting,* and determine the *goal.*
3. State and explore *alternatives.*
4. Gather *information.*
5. Explore *implications.*
6. Clarify *values.*
7. *Re-examine* goals, alternative choices, risks, and consequences.
8. *Decide* from alternatives.
9. *Generalize* to other situations.
10. *Evaluate* the process.

Behavior changing skills

MODELING

Modeling is a method of learning by vicarious experience or imitation, such as watching the performance of others. The research evidence (Bandura 1969, Krumboltz and Thoreson 1969) suggests that a wide variety of behavior can be changed through modeling. Common sense experience attests to the power of examples also. In the context of learning helping skills in chapter 5, we discussed the practical consequences of modeling theory for the helping process and the powerful examples set by the helper's behavior. Helpees tend to do what the helper does. If the helper uses colorful street langauge to express himself, so will the helpee; if the helper discloses personal data about himself, the helpee will be more inclined to do so also. One of the problems in helping interviews is that helpees do not know what to do and verbal explanations often do not help. If the helper models expression of feeling, this gives the helpee a clearer picture of what behavior is expected. Another problem is that the helper's behavior must be at a higher level of functioning than the helpee's performance so he has a behavioral model to work up to (Carkhuff 1969).

Role playing is another example of vicarious behavior where the helpee can see, through roles performed by others, what is expected. If he is fearful of approaching an employer about a job, for example, the helper can perform the role of an applicant (the helpee), as the helpee acts as the employer. The two then continue until the helpee sees other ways of acting in an employment interview. Then the helpee tries on the new behavior himself through reversing roles and having them critiqued repeatedly until he learns the new behavior to his satisfaction.

A third example of modeling effectiveness is the removal of fears by observing fearless behavior in a model, acquiring information about the feared object, and finally having a direct experience with the threatening object with no ill effects. This type of situation would be effective with fears of snakes or of making speeches, for example.

Modeling seems to be most effective when the model has characteristics of status, competence, knowledge, and power. If the models possess qualities similar to helpers, they are effective. Advertising methods take advantage of these facts. An implication of these findings for helpers is to discover which qualities are most attractive to helpers and then use them as guidelines for selecting models.

Modeling can be done by live, filmed, or taped methods. Although live methods have some advantages, such as maintenance of interest, filmed versions allow for more careful emphasis on the behaviors that one wants to model. An example of a helping situation with delinquent boys, which utilized live college age models, is the work of Sarason (1968). Adolescent boys observed special modeling of the following situations: (1) vocational planning; (2) motivation and interests; (3) attitudes toward work and education; and (4) utility of socially appropriate behavior. When the boys observed socially acceptable models, they improved their own planning skills and ability to think in socially positive terms. The models were attractive to the boys and role playing methods sustained their interest.

Filmed models have been used with effectiveness also. Hosford and Sorenson (1969) used audio tape and filmed models successfully with fourth to sixth graders who wanted to speak up more in class. Motivating teenage students to do the investigational work necessary to career planning is a problem also. Stewart (1969), using group models on audio tape, found that students improved their interest in career information and more actively explored sources of information after listening to the tapes.

General principles of using modeling are:

1. Determine which features of a model would be most *attractive* to the helpee.
2. Decide upon the *objectives* of the modeling.
3. Choose *believable models* similar to the helpees in age, sex, and race.
4. Decide if *live or simulated modeling* would be more appropriate and practical.
5. Design a *modeling format,* script, or role playing sequence.
6. Conduct the *modeling exercise.*
7. Discuss the *helpee's reactions* in terms of feelings, learnings, and suggestions.
8. Recognize that *informally we are modeling behaviors constantly* for helpees.

REWARDING SKILLS

At several points in this book we have described the reinforcing, or rewarding, effect of various helping procedures. This section will develop this idea as a consciously applied skill. The basic idea is that rewarded behavior tends to be repeated. Another striking characteristic of rewards is that a wide variety of events can have reinforcing functions. We can use reinforcement: (1) overcome behavior deficiencies (as in encouraging a helpee to plan ahead); (2) change undesirable behavior (as in chronic stealing); and (3) maintain present responses (as in encouraging statements of feeling).

Although the idea of using rewards to shape behavior is a simple one, there are some pitfalls. Most of the principles of reinforcement have come from animal learning studies in which they were deprived of food and water, which then became the reinforcers. Since human responses are so much more complex, rewards have varied meanings. In helping situations we depend mainly on words, which have different effects depending on the cultural background of the helpee. Praise words, such as "good job" for example, are used commonly, but soon lose their effect because of overuse, and because they have differing levels of potency for different people. Verbal rewards are most effective when the helper and helpee are working toward common goals. They are resented as blatant manipulation when used to influence the helpee in ways that are not in his apparent best interests.

Some *general principles* in using reinforcement as a skill are that the reward, or incentive system, must be capable of maintaining a high level of action over a *long period.* In other words, we want the learning to be lasting. Secondly, we want the reward to be dependent on the appearance of the behavior we want. We want the *desired behavior rewarded,* which is difficult in ordinary life situations because the reward is often badly timed or is given haphazardly. As a result, the undesired behavior is rewarded. Finally, the reward must be *strong* enough and given *often* enough for the desired behavior to be repeated. We also want the behavior to *generalize* to similar situations when the rewards are not present, as in being able to solve problems in other contexts. This reinforcement process is aided by using natural settings, varying the reward, and rewarding conditions systematically.

The *general strategy* for using rewards is to plan them selectively in a pattern so that the desired behavior is emitted in the form and sequence desired. This is called a *reinforcement schedule* or *contingency.* We apply these stimuli (such as praise) in the appropriate strength and frequency until the appearance of the desired behavior is as strong and as frequent as required. With children, tangible reinforcers such as toys and candy are used. Adults respond to money, usually. The strategy begins with finding the *appropriate type* and *strength* of reinforcing agent.

Using tangible reinforcers is very controversial since some claim it to be similar to bribing. This argument is not as relevant here because bribing has illegal implications for adults, or at least is considered dishonest. Bribery is "pay" before the act whereas reinforcers are given after the act is performed. It is generally conceded by writers on the subject (e.g. O'Leary, Poulos, and Devine 1972) that social reinforcers, such as praise, are more desirable. Tangible reinforcers have a place if they are *not* used: (1) to *control* others; (2) to reward an act required in *daily living;* (3) to stop undesirable behavior (such as giving ice cream to stop crying); (4) to *replace* intrinsic rewards (such as self-satisfaction); (5) to *affect* others *adversely* (such as favoritism with rewards). When tangible reinforcers are used it is understood that they are an expedient to get the desired behavior more fixed and that they should be reduced as soon as possible. It is hoped that more *intrinsic* personal rewards will take their place and that people of all ages will outgrow their dependence on "gold stars." We must recognize, however, that people seemingly never outgrow their need for praise and affection, so these usually remain through life as powerful reinforcers in the helping process.

Generally, it is desirable not to use "if statements" to get desired results because they imply doubt about the person's willingness or ability to do the task. For example, one says, "If you learn this vocabulary list, you can eat lunch." A preferred method is to say, "When you have completed this task, you can go outside."

A final word on strategy of reward is to *praise the action, not the person.* An example is, "I liked the way you helped Bob this morning, Jim," rather than, "You are a good boy, Jim, the way you help others."

The "Achievement House" proposal described in the previous chapter is an example of utilizing the principles of behavior modification described in this chapter. Such a controlled environment makes especially effective use of rewarding skills.

This process may sound very mechanical and manipulative, but remember that we are describing a behavior change technique used in an ethical context where these methods are used with the helpee's knowledge and consent. If we are interested in the effects of these methods on the group, we can use these same principles at a social system level. Individual performance can be made contingent on the group performance and vice versa. We may design double reinforcement contingencies for the person and the group. For example, we can influence the degree of support, cohesiveness, productivity, and level of responsible behavior in individuals and groups by planning a suitable system of rewards.

There are many opportunities to use rewards in helping interviews or groups. If we want the helpee, for example, to focus on feeling expression, our attention to these expressions, as well as overt praise, will tend to increase this behavior. If initiative in seeking information to solve his problems is important, there are many ways to show approval in a reinforcing manner. This discussion of reward should make us more aware of all aspects of our helper behavior which has a reinforcing effect on the helpee's behavior.

Reinforcement has a decided effect on the helpee interview behavior as demonstrated by Ryan and Krumboltz (1964). Using verbal reinforcers such as "good," "fine," and approval nods in decision-making interviews, they were able to effect significant increases in helpee deliberation and decision responses. Similarly, a study of rural youth in group settings done by Meyer, Strowig, and Hosford (1970) revealed that information-seeking behavior can be increased considerably in eleventh graders by reinforcement methods. They found also that counselors could be taught to use these skills very quickly.

A summary of rewarding skills in the helping process follows:

1. *Reward performance,* not the person.
2. Determine the reward most *appropriate* to the helpee, considering unique interests, age, and setting.
3. Utilize *social* rather than tangible reinforcers.
4. Apply the reinforcer as *soon* after appearance of the desired behavior as possible.
5. As an *ethical* matter, obtain the understanding and permission of the helpee when using rewarding methods.

CONTRACTING SKILLS

Contracting is a method for systematically arranging the rewards so that the probability of a response is increased. A contract is an agreement with the helpee which identifies the specific tasks both helper and helpee will perform in return for specific rewards. An example with a child helpee would be his agreement to get his homework in regularly for one week in return for a special privilege. With an adult helpee an example would be the helpee's agreement to do some "homework" on his problem in return for helper talk time. Helping relationships with mature helpees have informal contracts which run something like, "I do (something specific) for you and in return you do (something specific) for me so we can achieve our mutual goals." Formal helping relationships, particularly forms labeled counseling and psychotherapy, are judged to be successful in terms of the extent to which both helper and helpee carry out their parts of the implied contract to reach certain goals.

Characteristics of contracts are: (1) *Specificity*—the helpee knows what is expected of him and the consequences for doing or not doing the agreed tasks. He makes the choices so he learns to make decisions and to take responsibility for his own behavior. (2) *Impersonality*—the helpee is not emotionally obligated to do the agreed task, nor is the helper emotionally involved in his doing the task. Both parties understand the consequences of not fulfilling the contract so the whole issue of achievement is put on an impartial and impersonal basis. (3) *Feasibility*—the specified task must be in the behavioral repertoire of the helpee. If a helper expects the helpee to listen more accurately, the helpee must be able to attend for a sufficient time.

Although all helping relationships have implied contracts—understandings that both will have responsibilities to carry out—they usually are not formalized to the extent of writing down the conditions. Written contracts are constructed only when there is some doubt, as in the case of children, that they understand the nature of a "contract," or that they will respond with expected responsible behavior.

Formal contracts usually include statements of: (1) privileges extended; (2) responsibilities incurred; (3) bonuses and sactions for completing or not completing agreed responsibilities; (4) how and by whom the contract is to be monitored. Contracts are commonly made between parents or teachers and children whose behavior has resulted in a breakdown of communication or confidence. These contracts are often "negotiated" with the help of an outside person. This is one reason for helpers to understand the principles and skills in behavior-change contracting.

Some of the *conditions* to be determined before constructing the contract include: (1) identify the *specific behavior* that is *inappropriate;* (2) identify the *specific desired behavior;* (3) identify the *conditions* which *arouse* and *maintain* the inappropriate behavior (What sets off the behavior; what is he *doing* at the time, and what *rewards* does he get for doing it?); (4) collect *baseline data* about how often the inappropriate behavior occurs; (How often? Who are significant persons to him? Their influence?); (5) identify the *conditions* that *arouse* the *appropriate behavior* (What do the other persons do, or could do, to arouse and reinforce this behavior?); (6) determine *reinforcers* and establish a *schedule* of reinforcement; (7) *negotiate a contract* with all persons concerned and *secure commitment* to it for a specified time.

Both informal and written contracts are used commonly in educational settings where specific tasks are to be performed. Homme's (1971) manual is a practical guide to writing contracts in a classroom, but it applies equally well to family situations where helpers often develop contingency contracts between parents and children and between husbands and wives. Conditions usually included in contracts are: (1) Use *reward* liberally, even for small approximations to the desired behavior. (2) Rewards should be given *soon* in small amounts following the performances. (3) Contracts should be *understood* clearly by all parties and be considered *fair* and reasonable. (4) The contract should be expressed in *positive terms,* such as "Finish your homework, then you can swim," rather than negatively, "Finish your homework or you will not get that new ball."

A summary of principles for using contracting skills is:

1. Recognize a contract as an *agreement* between you and the helpee about the nature and conduct of your responsibilities.
2. Decide if a *formal contract* would facilitate the use of reinforcing conditions in a behavior change problem, or if an *informal agreement* would suffice.
3. Formulate the *contract* for the specified *time.*
4. Ascertain that all parties *understand* and *agree* to the contract.
5. Provide for *monitoring* the contract and deciding when the contract is to be *terminated.*

EXTINGUISHING SKILLS

Extinguishing skills are closely related to reinforcing methods since behavior gradually subsides and eventually disappears when it is not reinforced. Thus, the skill element for the helper is applying this principle, known as "extinction," in systematic ways. Behavior can be changed by discontinuing the rewards. If the helpee wants to change an undesirable behavior, for example, the helper assists him to identify the conditions that are reinforcing it and then removing or weakening them.

Characteristics of extinction are that: (1) *rates* of extinction are *variable* and depend upon the regularity of reinforcement, the effort required to perform, perceived changes in the reinforcement pattern, and the availability of alternate responses; (2) *avoidance behaviors* can be extinguished by prevention of punishing consequences; (3) behavior is *displaced* rather than lost since it can be reinstated quickly through re-establishing the reward schedule; (4) using extinction does *not guarantee* that more desirable behavior patterns will emerge.

Usually, after extinction of the undesirable behavior, efforts to elicit and reward desired behavior need to be undertaken. Behavior changes can be brought about most effectively by a *combination strategy* of extinguishing undesirable behavior along with modeling and reinforcing desirable behavior.

Methods of extinction include: (1) simple *removal of reinforcing conditions* (as in not attending to an overly talkative helpee); and (2) gradually *changing the external stimulus* for an undesirable behavior, for example, by exposing the person in small increments to a fearsome situation, where the fear is minimally elicited and the fear response is blocked. Gradually, the fear will be neutralized. One method for doing this is through "behavior rehearsal," a kind of role playing (Lazarus 1966). The helper and helpee role play scenes from actual problem situations. The method works well with helpees who want to be more assertive. In this case, the helper poses problems for the helpee around asking favors, making complaints, or refusing a request, in a gradual manner until the most difficult situations are encountered. Time is taken for critiquing the experience and for occasional modeling where the helper takes the role of the helpee. The helpee is urged to try the new techniques under conditions where anxiety arousal is least probable. The advantage of this behavior-reversal method is that it involves the helpee actively solving a close-to-life problem.

There are complex and still experimental methods for extinguishing avoidance behavior through massive exposure to highly noxious stimuli without injurious consequences. This process, known as "implosion," is not yet practical for most helpers. An example is helping a person to stop drinking by taking so much that he gets sick and avoids alcohol. Intensive imagery is used also to focus attention on unpleasant stimuli.

The main implication of extinction phenomena for helpers is to know how to change undesirable helpee behavior by removing the rewarding conditions. Does our intense attending behavior, for example, always reward the desired helpee behavior? Are there some behaviors, such as tendencies to overintellectualize, or to talk to the floor, that we would like to extinguish by altering the reinforcing stimuli? In summary, then, helpers can use extinction by showing the helpee how he can remove rewarding conditions for unwanted behavior. He can help also by neutralizing undesirable emotional behaviors, such as fear of crowds, by gradually exposing the helpee to fearsome situations and by helping him to avoid punishing consequences.

AVERSIVE CONTROL SKILL

This skill related to reinforcement and extinction involves a process of removing undesired behaviors through use of "punishing" or "aversive" stimuli. The principal theory of how aversive control works is that the punishing effect results in a conditioned fear which has an inhibiting or suppressing effect. Aversive control is used to help reduce undesirable and persistent responses which are self-reinforcing. Examples are self-punishing activities in children, and unwanted smoking, overeating, and drinking in adults. To be used successfully, however, aversive methods should be paired with a positive reinforcement program for desired behaviors. Usually, other forms of help are needed, since aversive control methods deprive the helpee of much pleasure. He must be unusually cooperative and desire behavior change intensely.

Elements of aversive control are: (1) Introduce an aversive stimulus at the *time the person is engaging in the unwanted behavior.* Standard efforts for problem drinkers, for example, have been to put an emetic with the drink so he gets nauseous and vomits when he drinks. Dire warnings of impending cancer are given to smokers when they light up. Temporary banishment from the group is effected for stealing property. (2) Develop a *positive reinforcing schedule for new behaviors* when the noxious behavior has ceased. (3) Be alert to *undesirable side effects* such as excessive fear arousal or unwanted negative attitudes toward the helper who suggested or administered the aversive stimulus.

Sometimes aversive consequences can be imagined with desirable effects. The helpee is asked to create the situation in his fantasy which is like the one he faces. For example, the helpee is having great trouble fighting with his demanding mother. He wanted to avoid his strong responses, so with the aid of the helper he could imagine his demanding mother and work out alternative responses to her.

DESENSITIZING SKILL

Desensitization is a method of reducing the emotional responsiveness to threatening or unpleasant stimuli by introducing an activity which is incompatible with the threat response. Sometimes this process is known as "counterconditioning." For example, fear of speaking up in class is associated with an incompatible pleasant and relaxed feeling. The unpleasant response (fear) cannot be experienced when the pleasant response (relaxation) is present. Most desensitization activities are concerned with introducing relaxation in the imaginary presence of anxiety, although it has been used with feelings of anger and guilt also. Occasionally, desensitization is used in combination with modeling and reinforcement.

Desensitization methods were developed initially by Wolpe (1952) and were refined by him and numerous other behavioral scientists. Appendix 3 includes a sample learning experience for the basic skill of desensitization. There are several steps in desensitization procedure: (1) discussion of conditions under which the problem occurs; (2) explanation of the method and its rationale, as a learning process, to the helpee; (3) relaxation training as described in chapter 7; (4) construction of an anxiety hierarchy; (5) working through the hierarchy.

Steps 1 through 3 on defining problems and inducing relaxation were described in previous chapters. Step 4, hierarchy construction, is conducted at the same time as the relaxation training takes place. Essentially, the hierarchy is a list of 12 to 14 anxiety-producing situations around the same theme, such as taking tests. These situations are ranked in his imagination from lowest anxiety at the top to highest anxiety at the bottom. It is desirable to go over the list with the helpee to determine the strength of each and the equality of intervals between items. They should be evenly spaced as to their potency in arousing anxiety. In the "fear of testing" example, they would be arranged from "waking up in the morning of the test" all the way to "opening the cover page of the test booklet."

The items in the hierarchy should be similar to, or represent, his real life experiences. They should be sufficiently detailed to help him imagine a clear image of the incident. Items should include a broad sample of situations where the feared incident, for example, might take place. The helpee should be able to see himself as actively involved rather than passively observing.

After the hierarchy is constructed and checked, the working-through process (Step 5) is begun. In the relaxed state the helpee is asked to imagine a few neutral scenes such as a path in the forest. Then, he is asked to project himself into the real problem and is given the top item in the hierarchy (lowest in anxiety). He is asked to indicate with a signal, such as raising an index finger, if he feels any anxiety. If so, relaxation exercises are undertaken again briefly. Then the helper returns to the hierarchy, reading the same item, and proceeding in the same manner through the hierarchy. If successful, the helpee should still feel generally relaxed even after imagining the most potent anxiety provoking situation on his list.

There are numerous nuances to the desensitization skill cluster. It is a sufficiently complex method to justify that you read more about it in the specialized readings at the end of this chapter and experience it yourself under an expert in the method. Hopefully, then you can try it yourself with a helpee under supervision until you master the steps.

The following list is a summary of desensitizing skill utilization:

1. Discuss *problem* with the helpee.
2. Decide if desensitization is *applicable*. (Desensitization might be indicated when a special isolated fear situation needs to be faced.)
3. Teach *relaxation* routines.
4. Construct *hierarchy* with the helpee.
5. *Test hierarchy* for rank order of *potency* and *evenness* of intervals between items by asking helpee, "Which is more anxiety provoking, A or B?"
6. Conduct *desensitization* by reading from the list, the least potent first, in about 30-minute sessions.
7. Check for relaxation and *repeat items* from the hierarchy until relaxed—stop and go back to relaxation methods if you cannot go on without anxiety.
8. Complete *entire hierarchy* (usually 12–20 items).

Outcomes you should expect
from studying this chapter

You now have competencies to: (1) describe the behavioral approach to changing specific performance; (2) identify the principal steps in the problem-solving and decision-making sequences; (3) demonstrate that you can help a person through the steps in problem-solving; (4) describe and illustrate behavior-changing skills of modeling, rewarding, contracting, extinguishing, aversion controlling, and desensitizing. Since the criteria of success with action skills are more apparent than with understanding and comfort skills, more clear outcomes can be observed. You can determine if your helpee did what he said he was going to do and to what level of proficiency.

Personal epilogue

This brief venture into the nature of the helping process and related skills has been like a conversation with you. At times I found myself persuading you to accept my point of view, and at other times, confronting you with a challenge to examine your beliefs about people and your style of helping. I did not intend to present an exhaustive formal treatise on the philosophical and scientific bases of helping. Rather, this book has been a distillation of my experiences with helpees, a composite of my dialogues with colleagues and students, and a summary of my readings through the vast literature on helping. It is my hope that these ideas will assist you to tap your resources, provide a framework for thinking through your experiences, and offer methods for improving your helping skills.

Helping relationships and behavior technology present a monumental challenge and opportunity to all people to make this world a more human place to live. I'm convinced from personal experience and observation that we must seek constantly for more effective helping modes and methods. We begin this process, I believe, with rigorous self-renewal followed by a continuous program of personal and professional growth. Evidence is mounting that our helping skills have little impact unless we are open to change, willing to risk, and are concerned about human welfare. The fact that helpees move toward their helper's interpersonal functioning level places a heavy burden on all those who hold forth as human helpers to be the best possible models of effective human beings.

Suggestions for further study

BANDURA, A. *Principles of Behavior Modification.* New York: Holt, Rinehart & Winston, 1969. (General principles on which behavior changing methods can be built.)

———. "Psychotherapy and the learning process." *Psychological Bulletin* 58 (1961); 143-57. (Basic article on applications of learning principles to the helping function of psychotherapy.)

BRAMMER, L., and SHOSTROM, E. *Therapeutic Psychology: Fundamentals of Actualization Counseling and Psychotherapy.* Englewood Cliffs, N.J.: Prentice-

Hall, 1968. (Ch. 12, Marriage Counseling; Ch. 13, Family Counseling; Ch. 14, Educational and Vocational Planning; Ch. 15, Problems of Value Choice.)

BUCKLEY, N., and WALKER, H. *Modifying Classroom Behavior.* Palo Alto, Calif.: Research Press, 1970. (A simplified approach to changing behavior in class settings.)

CARKHUFF, R. *Helping and Human Relations.* New York: Holt, Rinehart & Winston, 1969. (The appendix of Vol. 2 contains a clear account of the process of desensitization.)

GROSSBERG, J. "Behavior therapy: A review." *Psychological Bulletin* 62 (1964); 73-88. (Overview of limitations and possibilities of behavior modification methods.)

KRUMBOLTZ, J. *Revolution in Counseling: Implications of Behavioral Science.* Boston: Houghton Mifflin, 1966. (Collection of papers on the application of behavior change methods to the counseling function.)

———, and THORESON, C. *Behavioral Counseling: Cases and Techniques.* New York: Holt, Rinehart & Winston, 1969. (Papers on behavior modification principles and techniques.)

———, and KRUMBOLTZ, H. *Changing Children's Behavior.* Englewood Cliffs, N.J.: Prentice-Hall, 1972. (A manual of helping methods with children from a behavioral viewpoint.)

OSIPOW, S., and WALSH, W. *Behavior Change in Counseling: Readings and Cases.* New York: Appleton-Century-Crofts, 1970. (A collection of papers in issues and cases in behavior change.)

———. *Strategies in Counseling for Behavior Change.* New York: Appleton-Century-Crofts, 1970. (A theoretical and practical approach to behavior analysis and counseling strategy.)

RHODES, W. "Psychological techniques and theory applied to behavior modification." *Exceptional Child* 28 (1962); 330-33. (Principles underlying behavior modification in clear practical terms.)

TYLER, L. *The Work of the Counselor.* 2nd ed. New York: Appleton-Century-Crofts, 1961. (An overview of planning and decision making types of counseling.)

WOLPE, J. *The Practice of Behavior Therapy.* New York: Pergamon Press, 1969. (Detailed account of desensitization with illustrative cases.)

WOODY, R. Behavior therapy and school psychology. *Journal of School Psychology* 4 (1966); 1-14. (Overview of behavior modification methods for school settings.)

ZIFFERBLATT, S. *You Can Help Your Child Improve Study and Homework Behaviors.* Palo Alto, Calif.: Research Press, 1970. (A practical guide for improving school performance.)

A | *Exercise for learning attending behavior*

Introduction to appendices

The following appendices are included as examples of brief skill exercise outlines. These outlines include the essential elements in a learning exercise: 1) audience intended; 2) concept or skill to be learned; 3) purpose of the exercise; 4) learning objectives; 5) learning activities; 6) evaluation. These outlines are included as illustrations of skill exercises you can construct for yourself, not as do-it-yourself exercises to be followed verbatim.

Audience:

Students of helping procedures.

Concept:

Attending behavior is the helper's attempt to focus on the helpee's communication through nonverbal means, such as eye contact, gestures, postures, and selected verbal responses which indicate that the helper is in contact with him.

Purposes:

1. To communicate interest in the helpee.
2. To communicate understanding of what the helpee is saying.
3. To reinforce relationship interactions.

Learning objectives:

1. To demonstrate focus types of attending behaviors in a micro-skills learning setting (eye contact, gestures, posture, verbal response) such that the helpee reports satisfactory helper interest in him and understanding of his statements.
2. To demonstrate attending behaviors to other interaction settings in and out of class. These behaviors are natural and effective as indicated by feedback from fellow learners.

Learning activities:

1. Verify understanding of the concept after brief explanation.
2. View demonstration of attending behaviors.
3. View models of attending behavior in a helping process on videotape.
4. Practice skills in a round robin simulation structure.
5. Debrief exercise in trios.
6. Debrief exercise with total group.

Evaluation:

1. Learner obtains feedback from simulated micro-skills learning exercise regarding effectiveness of his attending behaviors. Learner continues skills practice until this observer and simulated helpee report satisfactory attending behaviors.
2. Learner reports to his trio on feedback regarding effectiveness of attending behaviors in everyday human interactions and helpee relationships.

B | *Exercise for learning paraphrasing skill*

Audience:

Students of helping procedures.

Concept:

Paraphrasing is a basic component of listening skill indicating the helper's understanding of the helpee's intent and messages. Paraphrasing is a method of stating the helper's understanding of the helpee's message in order to test that understanding.

Purposes:

1. To increase the accuracy of communication through aiding the helper to translate helpee language responses from less to more familiar, obscure to more clear and precise, and from complex to more simple forms.
2. To operationalize, in part, what it means to understand a helpee and to communicate that understanding.

Learning objectives:

1. To paraphrase helpee statements accurately such that he agrees in this exercise with three out of four attempts.
2. To use this skill in all human relationships as manifested by consistent efforts to paraphrase a speaker's meaning.

Learning activities:

1. Read John Wallen's paper "Paraphrase: A Basic Communication Skill for Improving Interpersonal Relationships."
2. Verify understanding of the concept and the method.
3. View demonstration of paraphrasing methods.
4. Practice skills in trio round robin structure.
5. Debrief exercises in trios.
6. Debrief exercise with total group.

Evaluation:

1. Learner obtains feedback regarding achievement of skill to level cited in objective number one above.
2. Learner reports to his trio later on his use of paraphrasing skill in everyday personal and client relationships.

C | *Exercise for learning desensitization skills*

Audience:

Students of helping procedures.

Concept:

Desensitization is a process of reducing anxious behavior by substituting a response that inhibits the anxiety. Stimuli that evoke anxiety are presented in increasingly stronger forms to the point where anxiety is no longer elicited. Anxiety is regarded as a learned response.

Purposes:

1. To reduce the helpee's discomforting anxiety in responses to specific real life stimuli.
2. To teach helpees how to control and reduce their anxiety without the presence of a helper.

Learning objectives:

1. To understand the components of hierarchy construction, relaxation procedure, and hierarchy presentation.

2. To assist the helpee to reduce his anxiety below the discomfort or dysfunction level by desensitization methods.

3. To be able to teach helpees to use desensitization methods without additional help.

Learning activities (through dyads):

1. Construct anxiety response hierarchy (which may be done as homework).

2. Review potency levels with the helpee (by asking "Is this item more disturbing than that one?"). Ascertain helpee's cooperation level, and continue only if he is cooperative.

3. Use relaxation exercise (standard progressive methods or a tape).

4. Present hierarchy items with lowest potency first, pause to let helpee fantacize on the item. Explain to him that he will try to replace his anxiety with feelings of relaxation. He should tell the helper by lifting his finger if any of the items still make him anxious.

5. Repeat the relaxation exercise as necessary. Repeat the same item or go on to the next hierarchy item as indicated by the helpee's ability to reduce his anxiety. He may be instructed to practice this method at home for a half hour a day.

6. Each hierarchy item is presented in the manner of 4 and 5 until all can be fantacized without evidence of anxiety. When anxiety shows in response to an item the fantasy is stopped and the relaxation exercise is repeated.

Evaluation:

1. The exercise is completed when the helpee works through his hierarchy with anxiety below the discomfort or dysfunction level.

2. The method is regarded as successful when the client can apply this method to his other real life situations.

Bibliography

BANDURA, A. 1969. *Principles of Behavior Modification*. New York: Holt, Rinehart & Winston.

BARON, R., and LIEBERT, R. 1971. *Human Social Behavior*. Homewood, Ill.: Dorsey Press.

BLOOM, B. 1963. Definitional aspects of crisis. *J. Consulting Psychology* 27; 184-89.

BRAMMER, L., and SHOSTROM, E. 1968. *Therapeutic Psychology*. Englewood Cliffs, N.J.: Prentice-Hall.

BRUNER, J. 1972. Nature and uses of immaturity. *Amer. Psychol.* 27; 1-22.

BULLMER, K. 1972. Improving accuracy of interpersonal perception through a direct teaching method. *J. Counseling Psychology* 19; 37-41.

CAPLAN, GERALD. 1964. *Principles of Preventive Psychiatry*. New York: Basic Books.

CARKHUFF, R. 1968. Differential functioning of lay and professional helpers. *J. Counseling Psychology* 15; 117-26.

————. 1969. *Helping and Human Relations*. 2 vols. New York: Holt, Rinehart & Winston.

————, and BERENSON, B. 1967. *Beyond Counseling and Therapy*. New York: Holt, Rinehart & Winston.

————, and TRUAX, C. 1965. Lay mental health counseling. *J. Consulting Psychology* 29; 426-31.

CARSON, R. 1967. A and B therapist types: A critical variable in psychotherapy. *J. Nervous and Mental Disease* 144; 47-54.

COMBS, A., ET AL. 1969. *Florida Studies in the Helping Professions*. Gainesville: University of Florida Press.

CORLISS, R., and RABE, P. 1969. *Psychotherapy from the Center: A Humanistic View of Change and Growth*. Scranton, Pa.: International Textbook.

CUNNINGHAM, G. 1970. Activity-oriented learning package for increasing individual counseling competencies. Spokane, Washington: Spokane Schools TTT Project. Unpublished mimeographed manuscript.

DANISH, S. 1971. Film-simulated counselor training. *Counselor Education and Supervision* 11; 29-35.

DARBONNE, A. 1967. Crisis: A review of theory, practice and research. *Psychotherapy: Theory, Research and Practice* 4; 49-56.

DILLEY, J., LEE, J., and VERRILL, E. 1971. Is empathy ear-to-ear or face-to-face? *Personnel and Guidance J.* 50; 188-91.

ELLIS, A. 1962. *Reason and Emotion in Psychotherapy*. New York: Lyle Stewart.

FRANKL, V. 1965. *The Doctor and the Soul, from Psychotherapy to Logotherapy.* 2nd ed. New York: Knopf.

GORDON, T. 1970. *Parent Effectiveness Training*. New York: Peter H. Wyden, Inc.

GUERNEY, B. 1969. *Psychotherapeutic Agents*. New York: Holt, Rinehart & Winston.

GURIN, G., VEROFF, J., and FELD, S. 1960. *Americans View Their Mental Health*. New York: Basic Books.

HAWKINSHIRE, F. 1963. Training needs for offenders working in community treatment program. *Experiments in Culture Expansion*. Sacramento, Calif.: State Department of Corrections.

HILL, R. 1958. Generic features of families under stress. *Social Casework* 29; 32-39. Also reprinted in Parad, H. *Crisis Intervention: Selected Readings*. New York: Family Service Association of America, 1965.

HOBBS, N. 1964. Mental health's third revolution. *American J. Orthqpsychiatry* 34; 822-33.

HOMME, L. 1971. *How to Use Contingency Contracting in the Classroom*. Rev. ed. Palo Alto, Calif.: Research Press.

HOSFORD, R., and SORENSON, D. 1969. Participating in classroom discussions. Ch. 24 in Krumboltz, J., and Thoreson, C. *Behavioral Counseling*. New York: Holt, Rinehart & Winston.

HOWARD, J. 1970. *Please Touch*. New York: McGraw-Hill.

HURVITZ, N. 1970. Peer self-help psychotherapy groups and their implications for psychotherapy. *Psychotherapy: Theory and Research* 7; 4-49.

IVEY, A. 1972. *Microcounseling: Interviewing Skills Manual*. Springfield, Ill.: C. C Thomas.

————— ET AL. 1968. Micro-counseling and attending behavior. *J. Counseling Psychology* 15; Monogr. Suppl. 1-12.

JACOBSON, E. 1938. *Progressive Relaxation*. 2nd ed. Chicago: The University of Chicago Press.

JOSLIN, L. 1965. Knowledge and counseling competence. *Personnel and Guidance J.* 43; 790-95.

JUNG, C., ET AL. 1971. *Leader's Manual: Interpersonal Communications*. Portland, Ore.: Copy Print Center.

KAGAN, N. 1971. Influencing human interaction. East Lansing: Michigan State University CCTV. Mimeographed.

KAUL, T., and SCHMIDT, L. 1971. Dimensions of interviewer trustworthiness. *J. Counseling Psychology* 18; 542-48.

KORNER, I. 1970. Hope as a method of coping. *J. Consulting and Clinical Psychology* 34; 134-39.

KRUMBOLTZ, J. 1966. Stating the goals of counseling. Monograph 1. Fullerton, Calif.: *California Personnel and Guidance Association.*

————, and SHEPPARD, L. 1969. Vocational problem-solving experiences. Ch. 32 in Krumboltz, J., and Thoreson, C. *Behavioral Counseling.* New York: Holt, Rinehart & Winston.

————, and THORESON, C. 1969. *Behavioral Counseling: Cases and Techniques.* New York: Holt, Rinehart & Winston.

LAZARUS, A. 1966. Behavior rehearsal vs. non-directive therapy vs. advice in effecting behavior change. *Behavior Research and Therapy* 4; 209-12.

————. 1971. Relaxation Exercises (cassette tapes, series B). Chicago: The Human Development Institute.

LINDEMANN, E. 1944. Symptomatology and management of acute grief. *American J. Psychiatry* 101; 7-21. Reprinted in Parad, H. *Crisis Intervention: Selected Readings.* New York: Family Service Association of America, 1965.

MAGOON, T. 1969. Developing skills for solving educational and vocational problems. Ch. 36 in Krumboltz, J., and Thoreson, C. *Behavioral Counseling.* New York: Holt, Rinehart & Winston.

MASLOW, A. 1962. *Toward a Psychology of Being.* Princeton, N.J.: D. Van Nostrand.

MEYER, J., STROWIG, W., and HOSFORD, R. 1970. Behavioral reinforcement with rural high school youth. *J. Counseling Psychology* 17; 127-32.

MICKELSON, D., and STEVIC, R. 1971. Differential effects of facilitative and non-facilitative behavioral counsels. *J. Counseling Psychology* 18; 314-19.

MILLER, G., and GELATT, H. Winter 1971–72. Deciding. *College Board Review,* #82.

O'LEARY, K., POULOS, R., and DEVINE, B. 1972. Tangible reinforcers: Bonuses or bribes? *J. Consulting and Clinical Psychology* 38; 1-8.

PARAD, H. 1965. *Crisis Intervention: Selected Readings.* New York: Family Service Association of America.

PHILLIPS, E., FIXSEN, E., and WOLF, M. 1971. *The Teaching-Family Handbook.* Lawrence, Kansas: Bureau of Child Research, Department of Human Development. Mimeographed.

PYLE, R., and SNYDER, F. 1971. Students as paraprofessional counselors at community colleges. *J. College Student Personnel* 12; 259-62.

REIK, T. 1948. *Listening with the Third Ear.* New York: Grove Press.

RIESSMAN, F. 1965. The helper therapy principle. *Social Work* 10; 27-32.

RIOCH, M. 1966. Changing concepts in the training of therapists. *J. Consulting Psychology* 30; 290-92.

ROGERS, C. 1951. *Client Centered Counseling.* Boston: Houghton Mifflin.

————. 1957. The necessary and sufficient conditions of therapeutic personality change. *J. Consulting Psychology* 21; 95-103.

————. 1961. *On Becoming a Person.* Boston: Houghton Mifflin.

RYAN, T., and KRUMBOLTZ, J. 1964. Effect of planned reinforcement counseling on client decision-making behavior. *J. of Counseling Psychology* 11; 315-23.

SARASON, I. 1968. Verbal learning, modeling and juvenile delinquency. *American Psychologist* 23; 254-66.

————, and GANZER, V. 1971. Modeling: an approach to the rehabilitation of juvenile offenders. Unpublished report to Department of Health, Education, and Welfare, Washington, D.C.

SCHMIDT, L., and STRONG, S. 1970. Expert and inexpert counselors. *J. Counseling Psychology* 17; 115-18.

SCHOFIELD, W. 1964. *Psychotherapy: The Purchase of Friendship.* Englewood Cliffs, N.J.: Prentice-Hall.

STEWART, N. 1969. Exploring and processing information about educational and vocational opportunities in groups. Ch. 26 in Krumboltz, J., and Thoreson, C. *Behavioral Counseling.* New York: Holt, Rinehart & Winston.

STRONG, S. 1968. Counseling: An interpersonal influence process. *J. Counseling Psychology* 15; 215-24.

————, and SCHMIDT, L. 1970. Trustworthiness and influence in counseling. *J. Counseling Psychology* 17; 197-204.

THORESON, C. 1972. "Learning House." Mimeographed. Stanford University, Stanford, Calif.

TRUAX, C., and CARKHUFF, R. 1964. The old and the new: theory and research in counseling and psychotherapy. *Personnel and Guidance J.* 42; 860-66.

————. 1967. *Toward Effective Counseling and Psychotherapy: Training and Practice.* Chicago: Aldine.

VARENHORST, B. 1969. Learning the consequences of life's decisions. Ch. 33 in Krumboltz, J. and Thoreson, C. *Behavioral Counseling.* New York: Holt, Rinehart & Winston.

————, and HAMBURG, B. 1971. Peer counselor program and curriculum. Palo Alto, Calif.: Palo Alto Unified School District. Mimeographed.

————. 1972. Progress report and current status of the Palo Alto peer counseling program. Palo Alto, Calif.: Palo Alto Unified School District. Mimeographed.

WHITEHORN, J., and BETZ, B. 1960. Further studies of the doctor as a crucial variable in the outcome of treatment with schizophrenic patients. *American J. of Psychiatry* 117; 215-23.

WOLPE, J. 1952. Objective psychotherapy of the neuroses. *South African Medical Journal* 26; 825-29.

YABLONSKY, L. 1965. *The Travel Back: Synanon.* New York: Macmillan.

Youth in the Ghetto. 1964. New York: Harlem Youth Opportunities Unlimited.

Index